991

Drawn by John J. Black April 1945

GREAT SIOUX RESERVATION

BLACK HILLS

NORTH DAKOTA
SOUTH DAKOTA

SOUTH DAKOTA
NEBRASKA

MISSOURI RIVER

Bismarck

FORT LINCOLN

TERRY-CUSTER COLUMN

SOUTH DAKOTA
WYOMING

SCALE

50   100

North Platte River

River

FORT LARAMIE

FORT FETTERMAN

FORT D. A. RUSSELL & CHEYENNE

WYOMING
COLORADO

CROOK'S COLUMN

CUSTER BATTLEFIELD

MONTANA
WYOMING

Powder River

Tongue River

Rosebud Cr.

L. Bighorn Riv.

Sheridan

Bighorn River

RIVER

YELLOWSTONE RIVER

GIBBON'S COLUMN

Billings

FORT ELLIS

Bozeman

Helena

FORT SHAW

Missouri River

YELLOWSTONE NATIONAL PARK

MONT.
IDAHO

IDAHO
WYOMING

IDAHO
UTAH

N

THREE PRONGED MOVEMENTS
IN THE SIOUX EXPEDITION
OF 1876

KICK THE DEAD LION

KICK THE DEAD LION
A Casebook of the Custer Battle

by
Charles G. du Bois

UPTON & SONS   EL SEGUNDO, CA   1987

LIBRARY OF CONGRESS CATALOG CARD NUMBER 87-50695
ISBN 0-912783-09-5

DEDICATION

To the "GARRYOWENS" — the men of the 7th U.S. Cavalry Regiment — who, since 1866 have served their country, at home and abroad, in the heroic tradition established by their first Lieutenant Colonel, Brevet Major General George Armstrong Custer, this work is dedicated, and especially to the memory of a latter-day Garryowen, the late Major Edward Smith Luce, friend and mentor, and one-time Superintendent of the Custer Battlefield National Monument.

TABLE OF CONTENTS

Publisher's Introduction xi
Preface xiii
Introduction xvii
Section I
    The Case Against Major Reno 3
Section II
    The Case Against Captain Benteen 27
Section III
    The Case of the Perfidious Petition 47
Section IV
    The Case Against General Custer 61
Appendix 85
Bibliography 93
Notes 95
Index 107

ILLUSTRATIONS

Marcus Reno 2
Custer's Message . . . . *facing page* 26
Frederick Benteen . . . . *facing page* 27
Enlisted Men's Petition . . . . *following page* 49
Payroll . . . . *following page* 49
George A. Custer 60

Publisher's Introduction to
Echoes of the Little Big Horn Series

UPTON AND SONS — PUBLISHERS will present Custer classics that have stood the test of time and are the cornerstones of any library devoted to the Battle of the Little Big Horn. The publisher's criteria for selection of books to the series includes: long out-of-print, expensive (when you can find a copy) and quality content.

Some volumes will be updated by the author. Other volumes will include corrections and additions the author, had he lived, planned to make in later editions. The volumes will be published occasionally, but always with high quality design.

PREFACE

On June 25, 1876, the greatest Indian battle in the history of the American West was fought on the Little Big Horn River in southeastern Montana. The combined forces of the Sioux and Cheyennes encamped there defeated the Seventh U. S. Cavalry Regiment and annihilated five companies of the regiment under the personal leadership of Brevet Major General George Armstrong Custer.

The first edition of *Kick the Dead Lion: A Casebook of the Custer Battle* was written in 1954 to challenge the critics of General Custer by focusing attention on the conduct of his two most prominent officers, Brevet Colonels Marcus A. Reno and Frederick Benteen, who attempted to exonerate themselves by shifting the blame to the dead Custer. In the years that followed three champions of Reno and Benteen: Fred Dustin, E. A. Brininstool and Frederic Van De Water[1], took up the fight, and lacking sufficient evidence to support their favorites, chose to defend them by employing the same tactic: namely, by attacking Custer.

In the 1970's, the motion picture, "Little Big Man," based on the fictional novel by Thomas Berger, caricatured Custer as a raving maniac. Perhaps it was more than mere ignorance that prompted this portrayal; it was, after all, the Age of the Antihero in which modern iconoclasts delighted in toppling our national heroes from their pedestals. Men such as Custer were dehumanized and degraded as objects of ridicule, their accomplishments disparaged, their characters maligned.

In the original introduction of *Kick the Dead Lion* I stated that "General George A. Custer died a hero's death in the service of his country. His was a soldier's death, quick and violent. Mourned by his friends, and they were many — reviled by his enemies, and they were many — he emerges today, in the light of truth, an honorable man worthy of his country's adulation. We Americans have long prided ourselves on our insistence for 'fair play.' With this in mind, let us sweep aside the cloak of mystery that surrounds the two leading detractors of Custer — Major Reno and Captain Benteen — and examine the facts with cold reason. Perhaps we may then agree with General Nelson A. Miles, one of the greatest of the army officers who served on the Western Frontier, when he said, 'I have no patience with those who would kick a dead lion'"[2]

Kick the Dead Lion has long been out-of-print, including the second edition of 1961 in which a chapter exposing the "Enlisted Men's Petition" and a chapter on Custer's own actions at the Little Big Horn were added. At the urging of a number of my friends, I offer this updated version of the book for a new generation of Americans, for this country of ours needs its heroes, perhaps moreso today than at any time in our history.

If my treatment of Reno and Benteen seems unduly harsh, let it be remembered that it was *their* malevolence toward the "dead lion" that made this riposte necessary. In a court of law both prosecutor and defense attorney engage in an adversarial encounter to prove their respective cases. The prosecutors of the past are no longer with us, but they have had their day in court. Though I speak for the defense the reader will note that I have also assumed the role of prosecutor, on the premise — learned from the original critics of Custer — that "the best defense is a good offense." So without apology this third edition is offered in the hope that a more realistic picture of the protagonists and their actions at the Little Big Horn may emerge.

Charles G. du Bois
Black Hawk SD

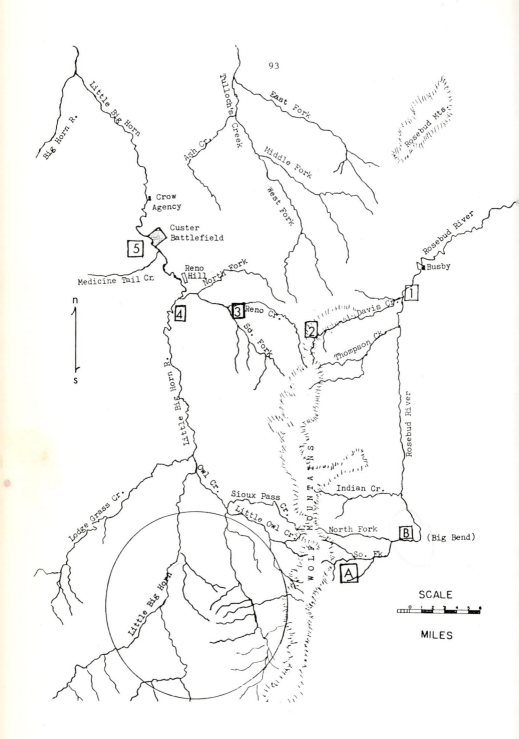

Big Horn R.

Little Big Horn

Tulloch's Creek

Ash Cr.

East Fork

Middle Fork

West Fork

Rosebud Mts.

Crow Agency

Custer Battlefield

⑤

Medicine Tail Cr.

Reno Hill

North Fork

Rosebud River

Busby

①

n
↑

|
s

④

③

Reno Cr.

So. Fork

②

Davis Cr.

Thompson Ck.

Rosebud River

Little Big Horn R.

Owl Cr.

Sioux Pass Cr.

Little Owl Cr.

W O L F   M O U N T A I N S

Indian Cr.

North Fork

Ⓑ   (Big Bend)

So. Fk.

Ⓐ

Lodge Grass Cr.

Little Big Horn

SCALE

0 1 2 3 4 5 6

MILES

INTRODUCTION

Some names are born never to die ... George Armstrong Custer was one of the few so destined. Though names may live on, life does end, and Custer's life came to a shocking finish on a hot Sunday afternoon in June, 1876, when a cruel angry bullet tore into his chest on the barren heights overlooking the Little Big Horn River in the vast and beautiful Montana Territory. Along with the Custer name, the Battle of the Little Big Horn also refuses to die and continues to challenge us to find the answers before its ghosts can disappear into history. George Armstrong Custer, in muted silence, cries out from the grave on that still desolate Montana hillside ... "Help me to defend myself for I can no longer raise my sword." And so we do.

George Armstrong Custer's military career was meteoric — a Second Lieutenant fresh out of West Point at 21, Brigidier General at 23, Major General at 25, commanding a division of cavalry in the Army of the Potomac, and in the words of the Confederate General Joseph B. Kershaw:

> One of the best cavalry officers that this or any other country ever produced.[1]

In the summer of 1876, after George Custer's death at the Little Big Horn, General Nelson A. Miles and his Fifth Infantry were ordered to patrol the Yellowstone as part of the Army's plan to capture the Indians who had killed Custer. After a frustrating and fruitless summer, Miles wrote his wife in late August:

> The more I see of movements here the more admiration I have
> for Custer and I am satisfied that his likes will not be found very
> soon again.'[2]

Why then should a man of such great military accomplishment
and reputation need to be defended?

The defeat of the United States Seventh Cavalry at the Little
Big Horn was a stunning and jolting experience for the
Country. The finest and most reputable cavalry regiment on the
frontier was decimated. Its leader, the Boy General of the Civil
War, who never lost a gun or a flag in that great conflict, was
dead by the hands of "hostile" Indians. The bodies of Custer
and his slain troopers had barely grown cold when the jackals
arrived. Someone had to be blamed for this terrible disaster and
who better to blame than those who could not answer and
defend themselves?

George Armstrong Custer's tactics at the Little Big Horn
were sound, given the set of facts he had before him. Indians
had always run rather than face an attack on their village by
cavalry and Custer began his assault convinced this would be
the same with the situation now confronting him. As the
situation became more clearly defined and the attack
developed, orders were given and orders were disobeyed. Had
Custer survived the Little Big Horn, there is little doubt he
would have preferred charges against his detachment commanders, Major Reno and Captain Benteen. Reno because of
his failure to obey a direct order, a critical part of Custer's
immediate plan, and for Reno's decision to keep two-thirds of
the regiment out of action when within the "sound of the guns."
Reno possibly could have been exonerated for his actions at the
Little Big Horn — his actions though perhaps poor in
judgement, were defensible. Benteen, the real culprit at the
Little Big Horn, emerged unscathed.

Benteen knew very well his actions — or inactions — at the

Little Big Horn, played a major role in the disaster, and he spent the rest of his life attempting to lead people away from the truth. Benteen was an experienced soldier, and perhaps overly qualified to be a troop commander in the Seventh Cavalry. He had led large bodies of troops in the Civil War, and after the War had turned down a majority in a colored regiment. "Ours is not to reason why ..." was not part of his makeup. He second-guessed his commanding officer's every move. Although apparently well-liked by his brother officers, he had no use for any one of them , either superior or subordinate. All one has to do to confirm this fact is to read the Benteen-Goldin letters. Most of the poison that flowed through the pens of Custer-phobe authors such as Dustin, Van de Water and Brininstool, found their source in these letters.

At the Reno Court of Inquiry, held at the Palmer House in Chicago in January, 1879, Benteen ridiculed Custer's orders which sent him on his reconnaissance-to-the-left, toward the Little Big Horn Valley, declaring the orders made no sense at all, when, in fact, he knew very well what was expected of him. Letters sent to his wife immediately after the Battle confirm this.
Statements made by his First Lieutenant, Francis Gibson, also verify the fact the mission had a purpose.

The indictable offense committed by Benteen, however was he idled at the morass while watering his horses, even though Captain Thomas Weir urged him to "move out." He then dawdled on the trail, disobeying all parts of the direct order he had received from Custer through Trumpeter Giovanni Martini. Overlooked by most historians in the evaluation of Benteen's response to the "hurry up " order received from Custer was when he received the order, he asked Trumpeter Martini what was happening when he left Custer. Martini stated the Indians were "skedaddling," which led Benteen to believe the information contained in Custer's direct order. In other words, Benteen placed more credence in the information received verbally from Martini than from the urgent written order he had just received from his commanding officer. Further evidence to confirm Benteen's improper actions may be found in the Benteen narrative wherein he states:

> He Martini informed me that the Indians were "skedaddling"; hence, less the necessity for retracing our steps to get the Pack . . .[3]

> . . . from the ford where Reno first crossed the beautifully blue Little Big Horn we saw going on what was eventually not "skedaddling" on the part of the Indians.[4]

> . . . we concluded that the lay of the land had better be investigated a bit, as so much of the Italian Trumpeter's story hadn't "panned out."[5]

Is it any wonder after such blatant disobedience why Benteen should not attempt to cast blame on the dead Custer for the defeat of the Seventh Cavalry at the Little Big Horn? Indeed, the Court of Inquiry, convened in 1879 to investigate Major Reno's conduct at the Little Big Horn, would have better served history had Benteen been its subject.

And so it goes on, with no apparent letup — those blaming Custer for the disaster at the Little Big Horn and those who have taken the time to find the truth defending him. No one suggests Reno or Benteen could have saved Custer when he made his final stand. By the time Custer found himself in his untenable position, it was probably too late — the damage had been done. Clearly, the failure of Reno and Benteen to follow their commanding officer's orders had a direct bearing on the defeat at the Little Big Horn.

One of the first books I read in my search for Custeriana, over 30 years ago, was *Kick the Dead Lion* I thought it then one of the finest studies and analyses of the major personalities and their actions at the Battle of the Little Big

Horn... my mind hasn't changed. Careful research always stands the test of time. In this third and latest edition of Charles G. duBois' *Kick the Dead Lion,* the truth is before you— well-written and documented by one of the finest Custer scholars I know.

W. Donald Horn
Short Hills, New Jersey

KICK THE DEAD LION

BVT. COLONEL MARCUS A. RENO
Major, 7th Cavalry
Courtesy of Custer Battlefield National Monument

SECTION I
The Case Against Major Reno

Perhaps the most controversial figure who participated in the Battle of the Little Big Horn was Brevet Colonel Marcus A. Reno, the only major on duty with the 7th Cavalry Regiment in the field at the time of the battle. It was Chance that placed Reno in the important role he was forced to enact. The two senior majors of the regiment were away on detached service, and by their absence missed the opportunity to participate. This quirk of fate placed Reno in the uncomfortable position of commanding troops in battle against hostile Indians, and it cost the lives of two hundred and sixty three men.

Reno served brilliantly in the Civil War, rising to the brevet rank of colonel. He was never wounded, but it is claimed that his horse was shot from under him at the Battle of the Wilderness. His experience in Indian fighting was nil.

Reno first gained prominence in the Expedition of 1876 two weeks before the battle. Twenty miles from the mouth of the Powder River, Montana Territory, he was ordered by the expedition commander, General Alfred Terry, to scout the area. With six troops of cavalry he was instructed to go up the Powder River to the mouth of the Little Powder, cross to the headwaters of Mizpah Creek and on to the Tongue River. From here he was to march northward along the Tongue to its confluence with the Yellowstone and rejoin the regiment which would march straight along the Yellowstone from the Powder. But Reno had his own ideas about what he should scout. Instead he passed from the Powder across the headwaters of both Mizpah and Pumpkin Creeks directly to the Tongue. From here he continued westward to the Rosebud River, which he scouted, moving upstream a few miles before turning back. He marched straight along the Rosebud to the Yellowstone and notified General Terry by messenger of his location. Terry was indignant over this gross disobedience, for it meant that the territory which Reno should have scouted would have to be bypassed, and might very well be the area containing the Indians. There was a rumor among the officers that Reno would be court-martialled, but the extremity of later events caused the subject to be forgotten.[1] Nevertheless, Reno had discovered an Indian trail on the Rosebud and it was decided that operations would be based on that information.

On June 22, 1876 the 7th Cavalry headed by General Custer moved up the Rosebud, following the Indian trail. On the evening of June 24 it was ascertained by the scouts that the trail turned toward the Little Big Horn River on the western side of the Wolf Mountains which separated the Rosebud from the Little Big Horn. The regiment made camp that night while the scouts rode ahead to a high point on the divide known as the "Crow's Nest." From this point they observed evidence of an Indian village in the valley fifteen miles to the west.[2] The information was passed on to Custer early the next morning. Realizing he was near the enemy, Custer decided to rest his column on the divide until June 26, and at that time to press the attack. Unfortunately, hostile scouts were seen observing the troops from a nearby ridge, and the report was made to Custer that his presence had been discovered. There was no course open but to attack without delay.

A mile west of the divide, Custer halted the regiment and divided it into four battalions. To Captain Benteen he assigned three companies and gave him the advance. Benteen marched off at an oblique to the left and was soon out of sight. Reno, with a battalion of Companies A, G and M, marched westward on the left bank of a small tributary winding toward the Little Big Horn with General Custer and Companies C, E, F, I and L marching parallel to the Reno battalion on the right bank of the little stream, now known as Reno Creek. The packtrain followed the Reno-Custer forces accompanied by Company B, commanded by Captain Thomas McDougall, and an escort made up of six privates and one non-commissioned officer from each of the other companies led by Lieutenant Edward Mathey.

Four and a half miles from the Little Big Horn the troops of Reno and Custer came upon the site of an abandoned village, evidence which further strengthened the credibility of the report that the Indians had learned of the presence of the soldiers and were leaving the vicinity. Fred Gerard, an interpreter, rode to the top of a nearby hillock and saw a band of Indians, numbering about forty, riding away in a cloud of dust. Assuming them to be the rear guard of the fleeing Indians Gerard turned to Custer and shouted, "There go your Indians, General, running like devils!"

This was precisely what Terry, Gibbon and Custer had feared — that the Indians might scatter and escape. Custer immediately acted on this information from Gerard. Actually, of course, the information was wrong.[3] The Indians were not running away; they were not even aware that troops were in the vicinity! But Custer had to rely on such information as he had, and an order was issued to Major Reno to charge the fleeing Indians and force them to stop and fight. There are differences of opinion regarding the orders given to Reno and it might be well to review them briefly.

Lieutenant Wallace, Dr. Porter, Major Reno, and his orderly, Sergeant Davern agree that the order was given to Reno by the regimental Adjutant, 1st Lieutenant William W.

Cooke. Fred Gerard, the interpreter, and George Herendeen, a scout, testified that the order was delivered to Reno by Custer. Actually, the point is of little consequence; regardless of who delivered the order it was still Custer's. A difference of opinion also exists concerning the phrasing of the order. Lieutenant Wallace said the order he heard given to Reno was, "The Indians are two miles and a half ahead; move forward as fast as you can and charge them as soon as you find them, and we will support." Sergeant Davern, who was perhaps in the best position to hear the words (except for Reno himself) agrees with Wallace generally. According to Davern, the order was "Gerard comes back and reports the Indian village three miles ahead and moving. The General directs you to take your three companies and drive everything before you. Colonel Benteen will be on your left and will have the same instructions."[4] No one else recalls hearing this last sentence.

The order was clear and precise. Custer left no room for argument or for deviation. His meaning is definite: "Move forward as fast as you can and charge them as soon as you can find them." Reno was allowed personal discretion only in the selection of his gait (although that was fairly definite: "as fast as you can") and in the time for charging the enemy ("as soon as you can find them.)" It was impossible under the circumstances to be more precise for the location of the Indians still had to be determined.

So Reno set out in compliance with his orders. At a trot, the battalion rode to the Little Big Horn, and crossing the stream, they reformed for action on the opposite bank. With A and M Companies in the line, G Company following in reserve, the scouts to the left and front, the battalion moved on down the broad, flat plain that characterizes the valley of the Little Big Horn, a lengthy stretch of ground ideally suited for the maneuver to which Reno was ordered: the cavalry charge, which always struck terror in the hearts of the Indians, and before which no Indian, no matter how valiant, would stand. It was over two miles from the point of Reno's crossing to the south end of the village, still well hidden by the snake-like, twisting bends of the river, its banks choked with timber and brush. As the first tepees came into view, Reno ordered the charge and the command swung into a gallop.

It is interesting to note Reno's description of that charge: "I deployed, and with the Ree [Arickara] scouts on my left, charged down the valley, driving the Indians with great ease for about two and a half miles. I, however, soon saw that I was being drawn into some trap, as they certainly would fight harder, and especially as we were nearing the village, which was still standing; besides, I could not see Custer or any other support; and at the same time *the very earth seemed to grow Indians, and they were running toward me in swarms, and from all directions.* I saw I must defend myself, and give up the attack mounted. This I did, taking advantage of a point of woods...I...*saw that I was fighting odds of at least* five to one, and that my only hope was to get out of the woods, where I would soon have been surrounded, and gain some high ground."[5]

Let's take a look at the italicized phrases in Reno's account, in the light of testimony offered by other witnesses.

According to Reno, he encountered Indians about two miles before he halted his charge, and as he drew nearer "the very earth seemed to grow Indians..." Finally, he infers that it was the overwhelming number of hostiles that forced him to halt and deploy his command.

George Herendeen, a scout assigned to Reno that day, was questioned on this point by Lieutenant (later General) Jesse Lee, Recorder at the Reno Court of Inquiry in 1879. Lee asked, "Did any Indians oppose the advance of the command?"

Herendeen answered, *"I did not see any and I was in front. The Indians were sitting still on their horses, seemed to be awaiting our approach, and did not move till we got near where the command dismounted. Then* they commenced making up and skirmishing out."

Herendeen was then asked if he heard any fire returned from the timber by the Indians, and he answered, "No, sir."

The Recorder queried, *"Was* there any returned?"

"I think not," replied Herendeen; "if there had been I could have heard the balls, and I heard none."

But Herendeen was Lee's own witness, not Reno's. Lee then asked the same questions of Lieutenant Hare, a witness for the defense and a staunch supporter of Reno. Speaking of Reno's "charge" down the valley, Lee asked, "Was his [Reno's] movement down the bottom opposed by any Indians? Were there any Indians between him and the point where the command was deployed?"

Hare answered, "If there were any, they were very few."

Yet Reno avers that "the very earth seemed to grow Indians" as he approached the village — that "they were running toward me in swarms and from all directions!"

Recorder Lee asked Herendeen to describe his own actions when the command halted and deployed on the skirmish line.

Said Herendeen, "We dismounted and sat down and watched the fire of the troops a few minutes. *There was no Indians near enough to shoot at so we sat there.* The troops were firing rapidly. We could see Indians on the hills, but *so far off it was no use to shoot at them.* There were two men with me, Reynolds and Gerard, and we proposed to all shoot at one Indan. We fired, *but all our shots fell short.* That was the only shot we fired there."

Lieutenant Lee continued, "At that time were there any Indians nearer to the command than that one Indian?"

Herendeen replied, "A little further down the valley than the one we shot at on the hill, I saw Indians, and after that they got closer, probably within three or four hundred yards."

"Swarming?" It scarcely seems so, according to this testimony! Yet Reno claimed that it was because of the great

number of Indians opposing him that he was forced on the defensive, thereby abandoning his definite orders to "charge them." But still a chance remained for Reno to salvage some measure of success. True, now that he had halted and eventually took cover in the timber, he had lost the initiative. The Indians, who by their own admission, were planning to leave the area and escape this sudden onslaught, now realized that Reno presented no danger to the village, and took the offensive. In his excellent defensive position Reno could now occupy the Indians on the south end of the village, enabling the forces of Custer and Benteen to continue their missions unopposed. Victory for the army was still in sight; a holding action in the timber by Reno's well fortified troops would serve nearly as well as a direct attack. Custer was somewhere near, Reno knew, simply because Custer had said he would support, and Benteen could not be far behind. How close Benteen actually was at that time will be shown later. It was only necessary for Reno to "dig in," exercise fire-control and wait for reinforcements. But history records that Reno did not wait. Less than half an hour passed from the time the troops took to the timber before the mad retreat began. In describing the defensive position in the timber, Reno had said: "The wood was about twenty feet lower than the plains where the Indians were, and the advantage of position there was theirs."

How does this opinion compare with the opinions of others? Benteen called Reno's position in the timber "a number one place." When asked how it compared with the position later taken by Reno at the top of the bluffs, after he had left the timber, Benteen answered, "I think it was a great deal better."

This from Captain Benteen, the man who more than any other attempted to prove that Reno acted wisely. It might be noted that General Gibbon, who relieved Reno on June 27, and Lieutenant Godfrey, with the Benteen battalion, expressed similar opinions.

From Reno's account of the fighting in the timber we get a

picture of a savage, bloody battle with men dying bravely as they try to stem the onrushing warriors. According to Reno, the position was "untenable;" the accepted definition of the word is "not capable of being held, maintained or defended." Were the losses as heavy, the situation as hopeless as Reno would have us believe, then his next action would be excusable — indeed, even laudable.

At the time Reno ordered his men from the skirmish line into the woods there were only two fatal casualties, Private George E. Smith whose horse carried him into the village, and Sergeant Miles O'Hara, mortally wounded on the skirmish line. It is believed that 1st Sergeant William Heyn had received a painful knee wound early in the fight, and it is known that Sergeant Charles White was also wounded on the skirmish line but as far as it is possible to determine they were the only casualties. In the timber, under the protection of the trees and brush lining the river, there were no reported casualties until Reno decided to retreat.

Standing in a little glade, Reno suddenly ordered the troops to mount. The order, given by voice only, was not generally heard. Those who did hear the order scrambled for their horses. One of them was the Arickara scout, Bloody Knife. Another was a trooper, Henry Klotzbucher who mounted at Reno's side. As the men swung onto their horses a series of shots rang out from the Indians at this suddenly visible target. Bloody Knife fell to the ground a few feet ahead of Reno, killed instantly by a bullet in the head, his blood and brains splattering over Reno's tunic. At the same moment Klotzbucher fell from his horse, mortally wounded, crying, "Oh, my God. I've got it!"

It was too much for Reno. His plans for the moment were forgotten. Hastily he shouted, "Dismount!," and jumped to the ground. By this time the troopers scattered further away in the woods were just receiving the original order and were beginning to mount their horses. As soon as Reno and those about him struck the ground the commander again ordered them to mount and he then proceeded to "lead" them away from the timber.

When later questioned about the absolute demoralization among the men as a result of that disastrous retreat, Reno answered, "That was a charge, sir!"

With Reno's second order to mount he created pandemonium among the men in the timber. Those within earshot obeyed; those too far away to hear the order were just complying with the previous order to dismount. The result: as Reno led his men out onto the plain he left behind the greater part of his command, many oblivious to the latest order, many frantically trying to find their horses so they might follow the retreating column.

Now, with two men dead in the timber (Klotzbucher was dying, at any rate), the position had become "untenable." Was Reno justified in leaving the timber? Let us again examine the testimony of those who fought there, discounting the opinions of Benteen, Gibbon and Godfrey who said the position was a good one. Their opinions were formulated after the battle was ended, based on their personal examination of the area. This is what some of those who were with Reno that afternoon had to say:

Herendeen, the scout, was asked how many men would have been required to check the Indians or drive them out at the time they were infiltrating the timber. He replied, "Ten men could have stopped them coming in at that one point, in my judgement."

Recorder Lee asked, "From your experience in Indian fights, how long could a command of one-hundred men have held in that timber with six or seven thousand rounds of ammunition judiciously used?" (It should be noted that Reno's battalion actually numbered 166 soldiers, scouts and civilians, less the few casualties incurred).

Herendeen answered, "I don't think the Indians could have

gotten them out of there at all, if they had water and provisions."

Had Herendeen's statement been unsupported, Mr. Gilbert, Reno's counsel, might have made some impression with his constant insinuations that the testimony of civilians was worthless. Reno's own witness, Lieutenant Luther Hare contributed some information on this point.

"If they [the Indians] had charged on him," said Hare, "the command could not have stood it but for a few minutes, but Indians don't do that. I think we could have stood them off about thirty minutes by using the ammunition judiciously."

Lieutenant Charles De Rudio, left behind in the timber with Herendeen and others, when questioned on the subject replied, "He could have held it as long as he had ammunition — probably three or four hours, depending on circumstances."

According to Herendeen, then, the position was practically impregnable. De Rudio regarded it as highly defensible, and Hare considered the timber temporarily safe. Had Reno held the position only as long as Hare's modest estimate of another thirty minutes, what a different result might have followed!

The reader will note that most of the witnesses appended their estimates with the provision that the ammunition must be used "judiciously."

Lt. Col. W. A. Graham, in the appendix of his book, *The Story of the Little Big Horn,* apparently believed that there was little or no fire-control in the valley fight. He said, "The men shot away their ammunition both recklessly and rapidly, and when the survivors reached the hills, more than half their scanty store had been expended." Colonel Graham added, "For this, Reno had been bitterly assailed, and not with entire justice."[6]

Why, then, when the ammunition packs arrived on Reno Hill only two hours after Reno reached the bluffs, was only *one* box opened, according to Lieutenant Wallace?

Here is the opinion of the fire-control exercised by the men of

Reno's command as witnessed by Lieutenant De Rudio. Mr. Gilbert, seemingly unable to recognize unshakeable truths, pressed De Rudio on cross-examination on the point of De Rudio's statement that the troops could have held out in the timber for hours. In doing so, he uncovered this revealing observation on fire-control:

Mr. Gilbert: "How long, in your judgment, would one-hundred rounds of ammunition last, if during the time the men were on the skirmish line, and the time they were in the timber, forty rounds had been expended, bearing in mind that you went with the soldiers to fire, not from the line, but from the timber at the Indians?"

Lieutenant De Rudio: "The men in the timber were firing slow, and only when they saw a good chance to hit some Indians. I don't think the men who were there fired over three or four shots apiece while I was there. They were perfectly covered, and there was no danger of being shot and they took time to fire."

Mr. Gilbert: "How long do you suppose one-hundred rounds of ammunition would have lasted in the timber?"

Lieutenant De Rudio: "Probably two hours, at all events."

Still unwilling to accept this information, Gilbert insisted, "A hundred rounds would last that long?"

De Rudio replied, "The balance that was left would, if it had been properly fired."

De Rudio, in a position to observe, seems to feel that proper fire-control *was* being exercised by the men.

So Reno left the timber, a position he could have held for hours merely by supervising fire-control through his company officers. But Reno had had enough; the sudden shock of the killing of two men near him (their deaths caused by his foolish order to mount) and the gory mess of blood and brains splattered on him completely unnerved him. His self-control was gone, his leadership — unsound as it had been up to this point — was lost entirely. His men were left bewildered, unordered and without that most necessary component of a military unit, a commander. True, the company commanders and subordinate officers were there, except for those who stampeded with Reno, but their authority was subject to Reno and they had to look to him for orders. When Reno left the timber at a gallop there was no course open but to follow. Reno was in command (nominally) and it was obligatory to follow him.[7]

Pistol in hand, Reno charged the Indian line which now nearly encircled the timber and all but covered the plain. The Indians broke ranks, as they always did when faced by a cavalry charge, and allowed him to pass, followed by a straggling column of men who seemed to have been infected by Reno's panic. It is one thing to be afraid, but quite another to allow those who look to their leader for guidance and example to see it. It is a miracle that any man survived that run through the Indian gauntlet. Out of the total of one-hundred and sixty-six who started the original attack that afternoon, 3 officers, 31 enlisted men, 2 civilians and 3 Indian scouts now lay dead in the valley.

Reno called it a "charge." One of the officers who followed him, Lieutenant Hare, was asked by Recorder Lee at the Court of Inquiry to "state whether any troops covered that retreat, if so, what troops and by whose order?"

Hare replied, "I don't know of any."

Lee then asked, "Did anybody appear in the rear trying to keep the Indians back?"

"I saw no efforts of that kind," answered Hare.

The Recorder then asked, "Was there any effort made at the river to keep the Indians back, or was it 'everyone get over as soon as possible'?"

The reply: "There were no troops covering the crossing that I saw."

Lieutenant Lee queried this witness of Reno on how he was impressed by the movement from the timber to the river; was it a charge, as Reno claimed, a retreat, or a run?

Hare, as faithful to Reno as he could be under the circmstances, answered, "I did not think it was a run, but it was a pretty fast retreat."

Perhaps the most damning evidence against Reno in the precipitousness of his flight to the hill, is this fact: *17 men were left behind in the woods* — 17 men who did not even receive the order to move out, or who received it too late to comply with any hope of success. Add to this the statistics of Reno's casualties: *two men killed and two men wounded before Reno decided to leave; thirty-seven men killed and at least seven men wounded by the time Reno had completed his wild hegira.* The retreat was a complete rout; men and horses dropped all along the way. It wasn't necessary for the Indians to be expert marksmen, which they were not; they had only to ride alongside the fleeing troopers and knock them from their saddles with tomahawk or rifle butt. There was no rear guard to protect the men from this assault. All such recognized military precautions were forgotten in the scramble for safety. And at the river the utter lack of supervision was even more apparent and more devastating. Men and horses piled into the stream in one rush and the Indians had only to stand on the riverbank and shoot the floundering victims at their leisure. Small wonder that so few survived!

As the troops crossed the stream they filed up a buffalo trail in a ravine that led to the top of the bluffs bordering the river and once on top, moved to a position about five hundred yards south, where they threw themselves to the ground in exhaustion. Had the Indians followed the men to the bluffs, not a man would have survived, but as the hostiles reached the stream most of them swerved to the north, moving rapidly downstream. It is common knowledge now why they left Reno at this time. General Custer and his five companies had been sighted in the hills a few miles north, threatening the lower end of the village. Reno was beaten; he presented no further threat to the Indians. He was now out of the fight — a force to be dealt with later at the discretion of the warriors, just as soon as this new danger could be met.

Had Reno stayed in the timber, Custer would have reached his destination at the north end of the village unopposed, Benteen would have arrived, and there would have been no "Last Stand," no annihilation of troops. But now the entire Indian force, estimated variously from three to five thousand warriors, swarmed to the ravines leading up the ridge where Custer and his men later died. It was not an easy victory, and even at this critical point could have been resolved differently had the other battalion commanders acted on their orders.

It would not be amiss at this time to comment upon the other reason why Reno decided to break for the hills. He had been promised in his orders that he would be supported. It was the failure of that support to come which prompted Reno to act as he did, according to his account. Major Reno, together with other responsible military leaders of that time and this, have said that Custer should have supported by an attack from the rear, following Reno. We take exception to this line of reasoning on the basis the maneuver was unsound and impractical. We must remember that Custer believed the Indians were running away, and Reno's charge was for the purpose of stopping them and forcing them to fight. Simply following Reno was unnecesary for he had sufficient force to achieve that objective without any additional help. This writer recalls only too well a lesson in tactics during World War II in which a similar situation was created by the instructors. The units involved were components of the Armored Force (the modern day cavalry) and we believe that the correct maneuver indicated by

this problem applied equally well to the situation in the Little
Big Horn valley. To support an attack in these two similar cases
called for a flanking movement by the supporting group —
precisely what Custer had in mind by turning to the north and
riding ahead of Reno toward the flank or upper end of the
supposedly retreating hostile column. Recorder Lee at the
Court of Inquiry saw its wisdom, too. He questioned Reno on
the subject. Here is the testimony:

Lee: "Had you any reason for believing General Custer
would not support you in any other way than by following in
your rear?"

Reno: "None, sir. In my opinion there was no other way to
support me."

Lee: "An attack on the flank would not be a support?"

Reno: "No, sir. Not under the circumstances."

Lee: "Did you not state in your report that he intended to
support you by an attack on the flank?"

Reno: "I may have said that."

That Reno did so state in his Official Report to General
Terry, dated July 5, 1876, is easily proved by this quotation
from that report: "After traveling over his [Custer's] trail it is
evident to me that Custer intended to support me by moving
further down the stream and attacking the village in flank."

The division of forces was a tactic Custer had employed with
overwhelming success at the Battle of the Washita in 1868. It
would more than likely occur to him to use it on the Little Big
Horn, and had he been given time to carry it out, the maneuver
would have undoubtedly succeeded.

Perhaps the true reason for Reno's failure lies in these words,
elicited from him by Recorder Lee:

"Did you go into that fight with feelings of confidence or
distrust in your commanding officer, General Custer?" asked
Lee.

Reno replied, "No, sir. Our relations were friendly enough, and if my own brothers had been in that column I could not have done any more than I did."

Lee persisted, "The question is, whether you went into the fight with feelings of confidence or distrust."

My feelings toward General Custer were friendly," answered Reno.

The Recorder was not to be put off. "I insist that the question be answered."

Finally, came the admission. "Well, sir," replied Reno, "I had known General Custer a long time, and *I had no confidence in his ability as a soldier.* I had known him all through the War."

During the Civil War both Generals Grant and Sheridan reposed their faith and confidence in the "Boy General," yet Major Reno "had no confidence in his ability as a soldier!"[8]

Reno described his actions upon reaching the hill as follows: "As soon as my men reached the top of the bluffs, they dismounted and opened fire on the Indians, in order to cover the ascent of their comrades, and when the remnant of my command was about me again, I quickly threw them into a line of defense."

Dr. J. R. Porter, the only physician to survive the retreat, was asked whom he had noticed first exercising any command or authority on the hill. He answered, "I first saw Lieutenant Varnum, who had his hat off, and he said, 'For God's sake, men, don't run. There are a good many officers and men killed and wounded, and we have to go back and get them.'"

Recorder Lee then asked Porter where he first saw Major Reno there. The reply, "I went up to the major and said, 'Major, the men were pretty well demoralized, weren't they?', and he answered, 'No, that was a charge, sir.'"

Lieutenant Hare, questioned by Lee on the orders or instructions given by Reno, answered, "I did not get up the hill till most of the men had got to the top. When I got there,

Captain Moylan was completing the skirmish line. Major Reno was standing there. I heard him give no orders, but he was standing there where he could supervise the formation."

So was the sagebrush...so were the horses *standing there.*

Ten minutes after Reno and his men reached the bluffs they were joined by Captain Benteen and his three companies. Let us pause here to examine the times involved. Reno opened his fight in the valley at approximately 3:20 p. m., when he halted his charge and formed the skirmish line. He moved his men into the timber at about 3:35, and at approximately 3:55 he began his disastrous retreat, reaching the bluffs at 4:10 p. m. Benteen joined him at 4:20 p. m., according to Lieutenant Godfrey,[9] approximately twenty-five minutes after Reno decided to retreat. Had Reno waited but thirty minutes longer in the timber, Benteen, following Custer's trail, would have arrived at a point overlooking the valley and would have been immediately available to assist him. Reno knew nothing of Benteen's movements, to be sure, but he did know that they had started with the same objective — to find the Indians — and would, therefore, both end up wherever those Indians were. But Reno had neither time nor patience for such deliberations.

By the time the Benteen column came up, it would be reasonable to assume that the senior officer, Reno, would have had a few moments to compose himself. Lieutenant Winfield S. Edgerly, with Benteen's command, described the scene at the time of his arrival:

"One of the first officers I saw was Major Reno. He was on his horse, he had lost his hat, and had a white handkerchief around his head. He was in an excited condition. As we came up, he turned and discharged his pistol towards the Indians."

Recorder Lee asked, "How far were the Indians away?"

"About one thousand yards," came the reply.

"How much beyond pistol range?"

Edgerly replied, *"Nine hundred yards beyond any effective*

range. I consider it done in a sort of defiance of the Indians."

At one thousand yards range, Reno could finally indulge in defiance!

Major Reno had told of his heroic actions once he had led his men to the safety of the hilltop — how he "quickly threw them into a line of defense." In the testimony of the officers just mentioned, he had done no such thing. If anything was done in the brief time before Benteen arrived, it was done by the subordinate officers and non-commissioned officers upon their own authority.

The testimony of Lieutenant Edward Godfrey of Benteen's battalion is interesting in its bearing on Reno's conduct on the hill. Here is an excerpt from the recorded testimony of the Court of Inquiry:

Question: "State fully and clearly your opinion of the conduct of Major Reno as commanding officer of the troops in that battle, in regard to courage, coolness and efficiency as far as these matters came within your observation or knowledge, and state the facts upon which your opinion is based."

Godfrey: "I saw very little of him on the first day or night. *I was not particularly impressed with any of the qualifications.*"

Question: "On the next day, during the engagement, how was it?"

Godfrey: "There was very little to do the next day except to lay and shoot. There was no supervision required, but what was done outside of the line was done by Captain Benteen."

Question: "State whether his conduct was such as tended to inspire the command with confidence in resisting the enemy."

Godfrey: "I don't think it was, generally."

Captain Benteen, tight-lipped and evasive when questioned on Reno's conduct, became quite voluble outside the confines of the Court. On many occasions he mentioned the damning fact that Reno had proposed to him on the night of June 25, to saddle up those who could ride and "get out." Benteen asked

Reno what he intended to do about those wounded and unable to ride. Reno replied, "Oh, we'll have to abandon those that can not ride." Benteen, in spite of his own imperfections was still enough of a soldier to veto this brutal proposal. Captain Moylan, on hearing the story, voiced the opinion of all decent men: "If what Colonel Benteen told me at Meade in 1883 was true, and I know of no reason to doubt it, then *Reno ought to have been shot.*"[10]

Later that night of June 25, Major Reno further proved his incompetence as a leader. The circumstances were brought out in the Court of Inquiry. B. F. Churchill, employed as a civilian packer with the expedition, was called on by Recorder Lee to testify as to what transpired that night. He told how he and another man, John Frett, a fellow packer, had gone to the packs to get blankets and food. The two men were accosted by an officer identified as Reno. The story actually concerned Frett, with Churchill as a corroborative witness, and Frett was later called to the stand to give his own testimony. Here it is, in part:

"In the evening, after the firing ceased, I went over towards where I had put the packs in the breastworks. I passed an officer but did not notice him until I was almost in front of him, when I turned and saw it was Major Reno. I saluted him and said, 'Good evening.' The first he said was, 'Are the mules 'tight'?' I said, 'Tight? What do you mean by "tight"?' He said, 'Tight, God damn you,' and with that slapped me in the face with his hand. Then he took a carbine and leveled it at me and said, 'I will shoot you.' At that time a friend of mine named Churchill, pulled me back, and that was the last I saw of Major Reno till the next day sometime."

Recorder Lee asked, "Did you notice anything in respect to Major Reno's condition there by act or word?"

Frett answered, "Yes, sir."

"Tell me what it was," prompted the Recorder.

Frett continued, "He had a bottle of whiskey in his hand, and as he slapped me, the whiskey flew over me and he staggered. If any other man was in the condition he was, I should call him drunk."

The questioning of the witness was then continued by Major Reno's counsel, Mr. Gilbert. "Major Reno smacked you in the face?"

"Yes, sir," answered Frett.

Gilbert seized upon this triumphantly. *"He was not a coward then, was he?"*

Obviously, drunken brawling was the criterion of valor in Gilbert's reasoning.

The farce continued with the questioning of Frett by Gilbert. "Major Reno was quite drunk, was he?"

Frett replied, "I would call a man drunk in the condition he was in."

"Would you say he was very drunk?", asked Gilbert.

"I would," said Frett.

Gilbert continued, "Did he stagger and stammer"

"Yes, sir," answered Frett. "His language was not very plain."

At this point in the cross-examination it becomes apparent that Gilbert finally realized he had hopelessly enmeshed himself in a position from which there was no honorable exit. His insults failed to shake Frett in any way, yet he relentlessly pursued the subject as though unable to find a suitable note on which to end it and extricate himself and his client with some vestige of self-respect. Again he pressed the witness. "He was pretty drunk according to your knowledge"

"Yes, sir," replied Frett. "Pretty drunk."

"Almost incapable of walking?"

"He braced himself against a pack," explained Frett.

Gilbert asked, "Where did he go after that?"

"I don't know," answered Frett. "I went away. I did not like the looks of his gun."

It would seem appropiate at this point to remind the reader that Gilbert was counsel for the defense, representing Major Reno. His line of questioning, or prompting, if you prefer, might tend to obscure this fact. The interrogation went on. Gilbert asked, "Major Reno was not only very drunk, he had a bottle of whiskey with him?"

The witness, Mr. Frett, replied, "It was either a bottle or a little jug. Anyway, the whiskey flew over me when he struck at me."

Finally, Gilbert concluded his questions. If there had been any doubts before that Reno had been "under the influence," Gilbert's cross-examination dispelled them beyond question.

Yet there was further corroboration. Recorder Lee called to the stand Captain Edward Mathey and asked if he had seen any whiskey in the command. Mathey replied, "On the 26th, I saw Major Reno have a bottle with a little in it. Someone spoke of being thirsty, and he said he had some whiskey to wet his mouth with and to keep from getting dry; to quench his thirst. It was a flask; I don't know whether a quart of a pint. There was very little left in it then."

So we arrive at the logical conclusion that Major Reno was intoxicated on the night of June 25, 1876.

The point has been raised by some that this fact is of no consequence. Colonel Graham, in a letter to the late W. A. Falconer of Bismarck, North Dakota, scoffed at the idea: "What difference did it make if Reno was as drunk as a boiled owl during the night? No one claims he was drunk while they were still fighting!"

Surely any military man must realize that although the firing had ceased for the night, Reno was still on duty as senior officer present, indeed, as the commanding officer in the absence of General Custer, of a badly beaten regiment, *still on the field of battle*, and in no way certain of the outcome. It was a time for serious determination on the part of the commander to carry out his full responsibilities to his men and to the uniform he wore, not a time for "drowning one's sorrows." A clear head was needed for the day which would ensue, not one muddled by overindulgence in liquor, and Reno's insipid actions on the following day of battle certainly did nothing to add credit to his already disreputable behavior.

Perhaps a better use for the whiskey might have been found in the make-shift hospital, to relieve the pain of the wounded, many sadly in need of some type of anasthetic. But a man who could callously desert nearly a company of men in the valley, then suggest abandoning the wounded, would certainly never think of any such humane use for the liquor at his disposal. As always, Reno thought first and last for himself.

This was typical of the character of the man entrusted by Custer with the successful prosecution of the initial assault against the hostiles. Small wonder the battle ended in ignoble defeat.

But Major Reno had other facets to his character. Actually, the following has no place in any narrative of the battle, yet it does tend to show clearly the pattern of degeneracy already evident, and for that reason it is included.

After the battle, with the regiment again in garrison, Reno ruled as regimental commander — this by the death of Custer and the absence of his superiors in rank. It comes as no surprise to learn how he wielded his authority. On March 8, 1877, less than a year after the Little Big Horn, Major Marcus A. Reno, 7th Calvary, faced a General Court-Martial convened at St. Paul, Minnesota, pursuant to Special Orders Number 22, Headquarters Department of Dakota. The charge: "Conduct unbecoming an officer and a gentleman."

In the specifications which followed, it was alleged that Major Reno had, on two separate occasions, attempted to force his attentions on the wife of an absent officer (absent on Reno's orders), and being rebuffed by the lady, Mrs. James Bell, then set to work in earnest to damage her reputation and restrict her freedom as the wife of an officer. His efforts finally came to the attention of the lady's husband, Captain Bell, who had the choice of killing the errant would-be paramour or satisfying his resentment by preferring court-martial charges against him. He chose the latter. The Court found Major Reno guilty, and, sentenced him "To be dismissed from the service."

On May 8, 1877, after the findings had been approved by the President, the Secretary of War announced that the Commander-in-Chief was "pleased to mitigate the latter, 'to suspension from rank and pay for two years from the first of May, 1877'."

Scarcely had the Reno Court of Inquiry of 1879 faded from the headlines when Major Reno again faced a General Court Martial. This time the setting was Fort Meade, Dakota Territory, the time was November 28, 1879, pursuant to Special Orders Numbers 123 and 128. The charge: "Conduct unbecoming an officer and a gentleman."

The specifications of this charge alleged that Reno had engaged in public brawling, assault on the person of a brother officer with a billiard cue, being drunk and disorderly, smashing windows...and peeping into the windows of Colonel Samuel D. Sturgis "between the hours of 9 and 11 o'clock P. M. on or about the 10th of November, 1879."

As usual, Major Reno pleaded "not guilty." As usual, the Court found him "guilty," and, as usual, sentenced him "To be dismissed from the military service of the United States."

This time, however, there was no presidential intervention. The President approved the findings and proceedings of the Court and confirmed them, appending:

"By direction of the Secretary of War, the sentence in the case of Major Marcus A. Reno, 7th Cavalry, will take effect April 1, 1880, from which date *he will cease to be an officer of the Army.*"

And there it was, finally! But for all practical purposes, Major Marcus A. Reno ceased to be an officer of the Army four years earlier, on June 25, 1876.

The famous "Come on. Be quick" message; Custer's last written order to Benteen. Benteen's translation appears at the top.
Photo Courtesy of U.S. Military Academy, West Point, N.Y.

BVT. COL. FREDERICK W. BENTEEN
Senior Captain of the 7th Cavalry
Courtesy of Custer Battlefield National Monument

SECTION II
The Case Against Captain Benteen

"Benteen is one of the most remarkable looking soldiers that the investigation has brought to Chicago. He has a very juvenile face and head, set on a most masculine body. To look at him casually, he might be mistaken for an overgrown drummer boy, but anyone who regards him intently or enters into conversation with him, will come away with the impression that Benteen is just as brave and manly a soldier as ever wore a uniform."

So wrote a reporter for the Chicago TIMES in 1879, while Captain Frederick W. Benteen, brevet colonel, was appearing as a witness at the Reno Court of Inquiry. And how close to the truth the reporter came in his description of the man! The "overgrown drummer boy" bore out the resemblance in ways other than physical appearance. His actions before and after that inquiry — indeed, during his entire lifetime — give evidence that Benteen was a man of neither maturity nor reliability. He had his great moments as a soldier, moments that have been magnified out of all proportion to obscure his failings. After the battle the general opinion of all, civilian and soldier alike, was that Benteen ranked as one of America's greatest warriors. The opinion was encouraged by Benteen himself, but there is doubt that he really believed it. His many shortcomings, his inadequacies were always with him, to plague and haunt him in his later years.

A Southerner by birth and heritage, Benteen forsook the cause of the Confederacy for a commission in the 10th Missouri Cavalry of the Union Army. His promotion was rapid, his bravery and skill undenied; but some mental quirk prevented Benteen from becoming what he strove so earnestly to be, a good soldier. Frederick Benteen was *insubordinate* — not on occasion, but habitually. It is wisely said that a man cannot *give* orders until he learns to *take* orders. Benteen attempted to take a shortcut, and never fully succeeded.

It is impossible to draw any accurate picture of the man; it is like trying to photograph a dancer with a "still" camera. Only one picture results from each exposure and every picture is different. So it was with Benteen. As one focuses the camera of the mind on him, he poses as a kindly, benign man, yet before the shutter snaps he shows himself to be cruel and irascible. Again, he appears tender, then brutal; lovable, then hateful. There is no consistency to the character of Benteen save one: *insubordination*. In this he was steadfast and immovable.

The object of the absolute and persistent hatred of Benteen was his commanding officer, General George A. Custer, the lieutenant-colonel of the 7th Cavalry Regiment. Much has been made of this bitter enmity, but little truth has been spoken. It has been said that the animosity between the two began after the Battle of the Washita in 1868. Actually it began with their first meeting, at the time Benteen joined the newly-formed 7th Cavalry at Fort Riley, Kansas, in 1866. In a letter dated 1896 to Theodore Goldin, a lesser charlatan, Benteen recalled that meeting:

"At my first formal call at his [Custer's] private quarters, he paraded his orders and books of the old Cavalry division in the Cavalry Corps, as if endeavoring to impress me with the magnitude and eminent success of his operations in it. I remember his orders shown me said, 'No gun has ever been pointed at the Division but what they captured it,' etc., etc.

"Well, the impression made on me at that interview was not a favorable one."[1]

Of that there can be no doubt! It was not the type of interview Benteen preferred. He had no opportunity to tell of his own brave exploits, overshadowed as he was by the greater accomplishments of a man who had risen to the rank of major general at the age of twenty-five! The brevet colonel had found his match, and he liked the man all the less for it. But whether the impression that Custer made on Benteen was favorable or not, there can be no doubt that Custer definitely made an impression, undimmed after the passage of thirty years.

What turns dislike into hatred? For the answer we must review the facts surrounding the incident at the Battle of the Washita that served to fan into flames the embers of hostility that smoldered in Benteen's breast.

General Custer commanded the regiment on that grueling march over the plains in the dead of winter, a march which in itself spoke highly of the commander and his men. At four o'clock on a cold November morning the regiment found the village of Black Kettle on the Washita River, and Custer prepared for the attack. The regiment was divided into four battalions, one of which was commanded by Major Joel Elliot whose instructions were to attack the left rear of the village in concert with the movements of the other battalions.

At dawn, the regiment charged. It was one of the most brilliantly conceived and executed battle maneuvers in the history of Indian warfare. One episode, inspired by sheer bravado, marred the overall success. Major Elliot, completing his charge, saw a group of Indians dash rapidly down stream. Turning to his men, he shouted, "Come on, men, a brevet or a coffin!"[2]

Once committed there was no choice for the brave but foolhardy men who followed the gallant major. Custer had cautioned his forces to stay together. The scouts had reported that the surrounding hills were full of Indians, and it would be sudden death for any of the men to wander away from the regiment. Elliot and the men who followed him rode swiftly out of sight of the command, still busily engaged in the fight. When the battle was over, Elliot's absence was noted. Captain Benteen, feeling a sudden affinity for a man who had proved himself as insubordinate as he, suggested that a party be sent out to find him. Custer, facing an impending blizzard and surrounded by an overwhelming enemy force, ordered the regiment to march back to Camp Supply. It was not until a few weeks later that a search party could be sent out to look for Elliot and his men. They were found, as it was thought they would be found, dead.

It seems inconceivable today that anyone could insist that Custer should risk more men in an attempt to locate one group who had ridden to their fate in disregard of orders. Yet Benteen maintained the feasibility of the plan for the remainder of his life. The incident preyed on his mind constantly, being distorted to the extent that Benteen finally became convinced that Custer had deliberately abandoned Elliot, when actually the reverse was closer to the truth.

In later years Benteen said that "when he [Custer] did anything that was irregular to me, or infringed on 'regulations,' where I was concerned, I always went to him in 'propria persona,' and had the matter adjusted at once." And again, in a letter to Goldin: "I never fought Custer in any but the most open-handed manner; always going face to face for it."[3]

With these revelations it becomes extremely difficult for Benteen to justify his criticism of Custer regarding Elliot's death at the Washita. For that criticism was propounded in the most under-handed way possible, by means of the infamous "Washita letter." This letter, written to W. J. De Gresse of St. Louis by Captain Benteen, was published in the St. Louis Democrat, and subsequently, on February 14, 1869, it appeared in the New York Times. In Benteen's typical style, full of high sounding, dramatic phrases, it reviewed with pretended horror the campaign of the previous winter, a campaign already acclaimed by the army as a great victory against uneven odds. With heavy sarcasm and bitterness, he wrote of Elliot's brave "charge" and his alleged abandonment by Custer. The letter, of course, was *unsigned*, typical of Benteen's "open-handed manner."

Naturally the letter came to Custer's attention. Benteen, in another letter to Goldin dated February 22, 1886, described the scene that followed Custer's receipt of the dispatch. Full of insubordination (regarded pridefully by Benteen), the letter presents an interesting sidelight on the man:

"At Fort Cobb, Indian Territory in winter of '68-'69, officers call was sounded one night from regimental headquarters. I sauntered up, the other officers being mostly there when I arrived. The officers were squatted around the inside of Custer's Sibley tent, (minus a wall), and Custer was walking around the center of tent with a rawhide riding whip in his hand. When all were assembled, he went on with a rambling story, stammering the while, that it had been reported to him that some one — or parties — had been belittling the fight of the Washita, etc., etc., and that if he heard any more of it, or it came to his ears who had done so, he would cowhide them, switching his rawhide the while.

"Being right at the door of tent, I stepped out, drew my revolver, turned the cylinder to see that 'twas in good working order, returned it lightly to holster, and went within. At pause in the talk, I said, 'General Custer, while I cannot father all the blame you have asserted, still, I guess I am the man you are after, and I am ready for the whipping promised.' He stammered and said, 'Colonel Benteen, I'll see you again, sir!'

"Doubtless, you can imagine what would have happened had the rawhide whirred! The 'Call' broke up, sine die, in silence, but no tears from whipping!"[4]

Those who were present at that meeting probably sat stunned

during this brief exchange. Undoubtedly Custer, too, was taken
aback by Benteen's revelation. There is little doubt that he had
held Benteen in great esteem prior to this incident, and it would
therefore come hard to a commander to learn so suddenly of the
enmity of one of his most trusted officers. But Custer, unlike
Benteen, was a man capable of forgiveness.

Some historians have claimed that Custer gave Benteen
further cause for grievance in their later association, but fail to
mention specific instances. If such was the case there is no
record of it. Lacking additional evidence the truth seems to be
this: outside of the Washita letter incident, there was no further
cause for enmity except that which was prompted by Benteen's
jealousy.

Benteen later admitted that "I always surmised what I
afterwards learned, de facto, that *he [Custer] wanted me badly as
a friend, but I could not be,* though I never fought him
covertly."[5]

And that is the man upon whom Custer bestowed the power
of life and death, June 25, 1876 — the life or death of Custer
himself, and the two-hundred nine men who rode with him!

At noon on that day, Custer assigned the advance to Captain
Benteen, giving him three companies: H, Benteen's own, D,
under Captain Thomas Weir, and K, commanded by 1st
Lieutenant Edward Godfrey. From the divide of the Wolf
Mountains overlooking the Little Big Horn valley, Benteen was
ordered to proceed to the left at an oblique, scouting the area
before him, as the regiment prepared to locate the exact position
of the Indian encampment still fifteen miles to the west. Custer,
with five companies, and Major Reno with three, moved down
along the banks of the little tributary called Reno Creek. The
exact phrasing of Benteen's orders is lost to us; only the Benteen
version remains, full of the captain's own interpolations. Here is
his testimony as taken from the record of the Reno Court of
Inquiry:

"My orders were to proceed out into a line of bluffs about four or five miles away, to pitch into anything I came across, and to send back word to General Custer at once if I came across anything. I had gone about a mile when I received instructions through the chief trumpeter of the regiment: if I found nothing before reaching the first line of bluffs, to go to the second line with the same instructions. I had gone, I suppose, a mile farther, when I received orders through the Sergeant Major of the regiment that if I saw nothing from the second line of bluffs, then to go on into the valley; and if there was nothing in the valley, to go on to the next valley.

"The ground was very rugged and we had to go through defiles and around high bluffs to get to the point to which I had been sent. I went to the second line of bluffs and saw no valley; and I knew the Indians had too much sense to go to any place over such a country; that if they had to go to any point in that direction, they had a better way to go. The last I saw the column was the grey horse troop at a dead gallop. I had an idea that General Custer was mistaken as to there being no Indians in that vicinity, and as there were no Indians there, and no valleys, I thought my duty was to go back to the trail and join the command."

Under oath, Benteen consistently maintained at the Court of Inquiry that he regarded Custer's orders as "senseless," calling his mission, "valley hunting, ad infinitum." But there is no doubt that Benteen fully understood exactly what Custer had in mind. The precise location of the village (if one existed) was still unknown; whether the Indians would be found in one contiguous village, or strung out along the river in individual camps extending for miles, still had to be determined; and finally, should the Indians attempt to escape to the south, Benteen would be there to head them off. In his subsequent testimony Benteen said that he was to "hunt up some Indians. I might have gone 20 miles without finding a valley." *The* valley now becomes *a* valley, and Benteen strove to conceal the fact that he had been ordered to a definite valley. There was only one — the valley of the Little Big Horn — the valley containing the horseherd seen by the scouts and therefore, the valley containing the hostiles. There is ample evidence to support the statement that Benteen was fully aware of his responsibility. In a letter dated July 2, 1876, a week after the battle, Benteen wrote to his wife:

"I was ordered with three companies, D, H, and K, to go to the left *for the purpose of hunting for the valley of the river — Indian camp — or anything I could find.*"[6]

In a later letter to his wife, he stated: "I was ordered...to go over the immense hill to the left, *in search of the valley, which was supposed to be very near by.*"[7]

Lieutenant Francis Gibson, Benteen's subaltern, said in a letter to the son of Captain George Yates, "His [Benteen's] orders were...to take his battalion to the left...and if he found any Indians trying to escape up the valley of the Little Bighorn, to intercept them and drive them back in the direction the village was supposed to be...Should he find nothing he was to pick up the trail again and follow it on."

And finally, in a letter to the New York *Herald*, dated August 8, 1876, Benteen said: "I was sent with my battalion to the left to a line of bluffs about five miles off, with instructions to look for Indians and see what was to be seen, and if I saw nothing there to go on, and when I had satisfied myself it was useless to go further in that direction, to join the main trail...No valleys were visible, not even the valley where the fight took place, until my command struck the river."[8]

And so it seems that regardless of how often and how vehemently Benteen challenged the wisdom of Custer's orders, no matter how emphatically and frequently he denounced them as "senseless," he understood them thoroughly and completely at the time they were given to him. The "valley hunting" was an afterthought inspired by his desire to confuse the issues at the Court of Inquiry.

It is impossible to reconcile Benteen's testimony at the Inquiry with fact. He admitted in a letter to his "pen pal" of the 1890's, Theodore Goldin: "The Court of Inquiry on Reno knew there was something kept back by me, but they didn't know how to dig it out by questioning, as I gave them no chance to do so; and Reno's attorney was posted 'thereon'."[9] (This was in reference to Reno's proposal to abandon the wounded on the hill, as reported in the previous chapter, but it was indicative of Benteen's unreliability as a witness).

Benteen's battalion marched off from the regimental division point about one mile west of the divide at 12:10 p.m. With Lieutenant Francis Gibson and a squad of soldiers riding ahead, Benteen continued at a left oblique for about one mile before turning to the right. At about 1:15 p.m. the battalion reached the main trail along Reno Creek having ridden a distance of about four miles.[10] Benteen, and some of his officers, later testified that they had ridden fifteen miles on the scout to the left, but the facts deny the claim. The battalion struck the trail just a half mile ahead of the slow-moving pack train which had started out nearly a half-hour after Benteen left.

Benteen continued at a walk along Reno Creek and arrived at what has been called the "morass" at 1:30. Here the battalion stopped to water the horses and to take a brief rest. The "rest" began to develop into an interminable delay, and Lieutenant Godfrey overheard one of the other officers remark, "I wonder what the old man is keeping us here so long for?"[11] Finally at 2:00 o'clock the pack train reached the morass and Captain Weir of Company D, apparently exasperated by the delay, ordered his company to mount and proceed along the trail. At this, Benteen then gave the order for the rest of the battalion to follow.

It should be noted that at the time Benteen arrived at the

morass he was about thirty minutes behind Custer. By the time he finally left that area the time lapse had increased to an hour, and the distance had lengthened from two to four miles.

We now arrive at the Supreme Error — the last message from Custer to Benteen, and Benteen's "compliance" with that order. The message, delivered by Private John Martini (or Martin as he was called), was concise. It read:

"Benteen, Come on — big village — be quick — bring packs. Signed: W. W. Cooke. P.S. Bring pacs [*sic*]."

This was not a letter of suggestions; this was a direct, explicit order, containing three definite orders and one qualifying, important piece of information which served to lend added emphasis to the orders. The three orders were:

1. COME ON.
2. BE QUICK.
3. BRING PACKS. (This repeated in a postscript).

The piece of information was contained in the phrase, "big village." Actually that was all Benteen needed to know. It meant one thing and *one thing only:* Custer had found the Indian village, the objective of the entire expedition. This was the information Custer might have expected from Benteen, or Benteen from Custer, depending on which column sighted the enemy first. This was fully confirmed by the Court of Inquiry, when Recorder Lee questioned Benteen:

Question: "When two columns such as yours and General Custer's are in quest of Indians, would it not be the duty of the one which found the Indians to notify the other?"

Answer: "Certainly."

Lieutenant Lee seized upon the admission to prove the point he was trying to establish. "Did you not receive such notification from General Custer at the hands of Trumpeter Martin?"

Benteen, realizing the implications of the question, was at a loss for a reply. Hurriedly, he fought for time. "I received an order to 'Come on, be quick, big village — bring packs. Bring packs.' He then had found —"

Suddenly he broke off in mid-sentence, aware of his admission. He continued, "I wish to say, before the order reached me, that I believe that General Custer and his whole command were dead."

The absolute absurdity of this statement is hardly worthy of comment. It is obvious that this "spur of the moment" speech, blurted out in an effort to extricate himself from a delicate and self-incriminating position was intended merely to throw the Recorder off the track, as he seemed to be getting too close to the truth. Apparently it succeeded, for Lee did not press the witness further, probably realizing that the Inquiry was to investigate the conduct of Major Reno, not Captain Benteen.

So Benteen had received the information that Custer had found the Indian Village. His orders to scout to the left (which he had already abandoned) were rescinded. Had the message from Custer contained only the words, "Benteen, big village" it would have been sufficient. The Indians were discovered; it was now incumbent upon Benteen to rejoin Custer post-haste. But the orders were even more explicit:

1. "COME ON." This order has but one meaning: Rejoin Custer. Benteen did nothing.

2. "BE QUICK." This is self-explanatory, but how did Benteen comply? Here's the testimony of Benteen from the Court of Inquiry:

Question: "After you received the order at the hands of Trumpeter Martin, was the gait of the command increased? And if not, why not?"

Answer: "I don't think that the gait was increased, as we were going as fast as we could without doing a gallop, but I gave the command 'Trot.' I don't think it increased the gait at all."

Recorder Lee questioned Lieutenant Winfield S. Edgerly who was with Company D under Captain Weir, with the Benteen battalion:

Question: "What was the gait you traveled after leaving the waterhole?"

Answer: "A fast walk. All the distance. Captain Benteen had a very fast walking horse and traveled as fast as he could walk all the time."

Question: "After Trumpeter Martin arrived, what was the gait?"

Answer: "The same."

It might be interjected here that there is an intermediate gait between a fast walk and a gallop, namely, a trot. Benteen said he gave the order to trot, but that it did not increase the gait at all. Edgerly maintained the gait was the same, a fast walk, and fails to mention any order to trot.

3. "BRING PACKS." Certainly there can be little doubt what Custer meant by asking for the packs, but perhaps a word of explanation would be in order. The pack train, commanded by Captain McDougall, with Lieutenant Mathey in charge of the escort, included a number of pack mules who carried only food and ammunition for the regiment. Some historians have made much of the fact that Martin, in a later account, said that Custer told him personally to tell Benteen to "bring the *ammunition* packs," and that Lieutenant W. W. Cooke, the Adjutant, who wrote the message, omitted the word "ammunition," This, they claim, excuses Benteen for not acting upon it, inasmuch as he could not know whether Custer wanted the *food* or the *ammunition*. Such specious reasoning borders on absurdity; surely Benteen knew that Custer was not contemplating a picnic! If he asked for the packs, after announcing the discovery of the enemy, he could only mean ammunition. Any other idea is ridiculous.

The written order brought by Martin was preceded by an

oral message, brought by Sergeant Daniel Kanipe of Company C, to "hurry up the packs" and "bring the pack train straight across to high ground."[12] Although this order was directed to Captain McDougall, Kanipe did stop and speak to Benteen on his way, and years later, in an interview conducted by Walter Camp, Kanipe said that his verbal orders included this: "If you see Benteen tell him to come on quick — a big Indian camp."[13] This information was never brought out at the Court of Inquiry, and it is not known if Kanipe did pass on this message when he met Benteen. It *is* known, however, that Kanipe did say to Benteen: "They want you up there as quick as you can get there — they have struck a big Indian camp."[14] This information, given both verbally and written, should have conveyed some sense of urgency to Benteen. who, nevertheless, continued his march at a walk.

Lieutenant Edgerly was also questioned on Benteen's reaction to Martin's message from Custer. He described it in these words:

"When we had gone about a mile [from the Lone Tepee on Reno Creek], Trumpeter Martin came along with the written message to Captain Benteen, signed by Lieutenant Cooke as Adjutant for General Custer. That order was shown to Captain Weir and myself . . . The remark was made by someone, either by Captain Weir or myself, that he [Custer] could not possibly want us to go for the packs, as Captain McDougall was there and would bring them up. There was no halt or delay, but we went on, Captain Benteen putting the order in his pocket."

It is difficult to understand Edgerly's reasoning, The order read: "Benteen . . . bring packs." Yet Edgerly, with the Benteen Battalion, said Custer "could not *possibly* want *us* to go for the packs!" Then why did he suppose Custer had addressed the message to Benteen? Of course Custer knew that McDougall, not Benteen, was in charge of the pack train; after all, it was Custer who assigned the pack train to McDougall.

Had he wanted McDougall to bring the pack train he would
have worded the message to that effect, but he wanted
Benteen's *battalion and the packs.* Through Sergeant Kanipe,
Custer had already ordered McDougall to "hurry the pack
train;" the written order to Benteen could only mean that his
battalion was to accompany McDougall and the pack train so
that all these personnel could come to Custer as one unit, rather
than as two separate groups.

This may have been the reasoning behind Recorder Lee's
next question. "At the time you received the order in regard to
the pack train, did you consider it necessary to take your
command and go and bring the pack train up?"

Benteen replied, "I did not consider it necessary at all,
because the Indians could not get to the pack train without
coming by me."

(The order said, "bring packs," not "*protect* them.")

As yet the order remained to be carried out, but Benteen
simply proceeded along at the same gait, and left the order in
the hands of Captain McDougall — or did he?

According to the Court record, Trumpeter Martin said that
Benteen sent him back to McDougall. Benteen denied this, and
it was not until Colonel W. A. Graham published Martin's story
in 1923, after a personal interview with Martin, that the record
was set straight. Martin told Graham: " By this time Captain
Weir had come up to us, and Colonel Benteen handed the
message to him to read and told me to join my company
[Benteen's own Company H].

"*He didn't give me any order to Captain McDougall,* who was
in command of the rear guard, *or to Lieutenant Mathey,* who had
the packs. I told them so at Chicago in 1879, when they had the
court of inquiry, but I didn't speak English so good then, and
they misunderstood me and made the report of my testimony
show that I took an order to Captain McDougall. But this is a
mistake ... I joined my troop and rode on with them."[15]

Who then *did* notify the pack train that Custer wanted the packs?

Recorder Lee asked Captain McDougall, "Did you receive any orders during that march from the place where you received General Custer's order [that is, from the divide] till you reached Major Reno's command on the hill?"

McDougall answered, "No, sir; only Lieutenant Mathey said the engagement was going on."

Lee then questioned Mathey: "Did you receive orders from General Custer, or Major Reno or Captain Benteen on that march?"

"No, sir," replied Mathey. "Only such as I received from Captain McDougall."

"Did any sergeant report to you with orders?", continued Lee.

Mathey answered, "No, sir."

The conclusion is inescapable: *no one* passed the order on to the pack train. Sergeant Kanipe, who was sent by Custer with the verbal order to "hurry up the packs," said in a 1908 interview that he "met McDougall" after passing Benteen, but did not explicitly state that he passed on Custer's message, and here both McDougall and Mathey, the only two officers with the pack train, say they never received any such message from anyone. As for the written order carried by Martin and addressed specifically to Benteen, nothing was done in response. The order was received and read by Benteen, shown to Weir and Edgerly, then *pocketed and ignored by Benteen.*

There are those who claim that Benteen acted in good faith and, in essence, did carry out his orders to the best of his ability. After all, they argue, did not Benteen proceed along Custer's trail, the pack train following? There is no question that he did, but was it deliberate? Benteen maintained that it was, inferring that he had intended to go on to Custer as ordered, but felt his presence was needed more acutely on Reno hill. However, the fact that he remained with Reno until some time after the pack train arrived casts suspicion on Benteen's "honorable intentions."

The Benteen column moved on to Reno hill. Assuredly it did not know it was going there, nor for what purpose. Reno had charged and retreated, and approximately ten minutes after Reno's men reached the hill, Benteen arrived with his battalion. At that time there was little or no action there. Benteen immediately took charge of the entire command until Reno was able to function again as an officer. One of Benteen's first actions was to show Reno the written order he had received from Custer, and he asked Reno where the general had gone. Reno replied that he did not know; that Custer had promised to support him and had not done so.

At this point it would be well to establish a rule of military procedure. When Benteen passed Custer's order on to Reno, was Reno — the senior officer present — then obligated to carry it out?

According to the late Major Edward S. Luce, a former member of the 7th Cavalry and an authority on the Custer Battle, the order remained Benteen's to carry out. Major Luce asserted that only Custer could rescind the order. Benteen would have been justified in ignoring it only if he knew defintely that Custer was dead. Custer was most certainly alive at that time, but had he not been Benteen could not have known it. Benteen cannot be blamed for stopping to aid the bewildered Reno, but once that was done, it was his duty to carry out his mission. This he did not do, although what happened later at Weir Point would, on the surface, indicate that he at least attempted it.

The findings of the Reno Court of Inquiry were as follows: "...while subordinates, in some instances, did more for the safety of the command by brilliant displays of courage than did

Major Reno, there was nothing in his conduct which requires animadversion from this Court."

Substitute the name of Captain Benteen for that of Major Reno and this finding will serve equally well as a summary of the fiasco at Weir Point. Here Benteen had a real opportunity to display his military prowess, so long and so loudly "ballyhooed" by his supporters, but he failed to take advantage of it. Had it not been for Captain Weir it is doubtful that *any* effort would have been made to relieve Custer, and had it not been for Lieutenant Godfrey, the entire episode might have resulted in a panic-stricken rout at least equal to Reno's retreat in the valley.

Captain Weir, a brevet lieutenant-colonel, must be commended for his attempt to aid Custer. As a troop commander in the Benteen battalion he was under the same obligation as Benteen to obey the written order from Custer. Having been shown the order and aware of the fact that Benteen had no intention of obeying it, he was fully justified in setting out with his Company. Once he had left, the rest of the regiment decided to follow in a most disorderly and unmilitary fashion. When the troops had gathered on the high ridges of Weir Point, a mile and a half north of Reno hill, the Custer Battlefield was in view, three miles further north, but Custer and his men were not visible. That there was action of the field, nearly all agreed. In viewing the field Lietenant Godfrey said later, "the conclusion was arrived at that Custer had been repulsed and the firing heard was the parting shots of the rear guard."[16]

In justice to Reno and Benteen it must be noted that they had no knowledge of the precariousness of Custer's position, and no blame can be attached to Benteen for not *seeing* Custer. That was probably a physical impossibility, due to the dust in the area. But Benteen's contention that the field of battle itself was not visible is difficult to accept. At the Court of Inquiry Benteen stated: "Some of the officers say that the battlefield was in sight but I know positively that it is not, having gone over it two or three times since." However, an examination of the field will show that the field *is* visible, even to the naked eye, and it must be remembered that the officers carried field glasses.

This was typical of Benteen's physical "incapabilities." He also claimed, as did Reno, that no firing could be heard from Custer while he and the others were loitering on Reno Hill. The Recorder at the Inquiry, after hearing the other officers testify that they did hear firing, seemed to take it for granted that Benteen had also, but he reckoned without that doughty warrior's penchant for individuality.

Recorder Lee asked, "With regard to the length of time you heard firing from General Custer's battlefield as it was afterwards ascertained to be —."

Benteen broke in with, "I heard none."

Gerard, Herendeen and DeRudio, left behind in the timber after Reno's retreat, all testified that they heard the firing from Custer hill. But what of those with Reno and Benteen?

Lieutenant Edgerly, who came up with Benteen, stated, "Shortly after I got to the hill, almost immediately, I heard firing and remarked it. Heavy firing, by volleys, down the creek. Captain Weir came to me and said General Custer was engaged, and we ought to go down. I said I thought so too. He went away walking up and down rather anxiously. I heard the firing plainly."

He went on to explain that his first sergeant also came up to him and commented on the firing, and then told of Weir's decision to move out to Custer's aid.

Lieutenant Godfrey's testimony bore out Edgerly and the others He was asked if he heard any firing and if so, how soon after his arrival with Benteen's battalion on Reno hill. He replied, "I can't recollect the time exactly except that it was after Lieutenant Hare had returned from going after the packs that we heard firing from below. I heard two distinct volleys. Still they sounded a long distance off. Then we heard scattering shots afterwards, not very heavy."

Lee asked, "What remark was made about the firing?"

Godfrey answered, 'Lieutenant Hare and myself were together and I called his attention to it ... I asked him if he heard that firing. The supposition was it was done by General Custer and his command."

"Was that firing of volleys loud enough to be heard by the command generally?"

"I think so," replied Godfrey.

Lee pressed the witness. 'What reason have you for thinking so?"

"I was about as far away from it as anybody in the command," said Godfrey, "and besides, *I am a little deaf naturally.*"

"Were you at that time?" asked Lee.

"Yes, sir," came the reply.

We know that Benteen was not totally deaf. The obvious conclusion, then, is that Benteen lied, or at least closed his ears to the firing.

Major Reno also denied hearing the firing when questioned at the Inquiry. Yet in his Official Report of July 5, 1876, he wrote, "We had heard firing in that direction and *knew it could only be Custer.*"

There is little to be gained — though much more could be said — in dwelling on the subject of action, or inaction, on Weir Point. The fact remains that the forces who went there, adequate enough in number to follow through to Custer, were not sufficiently supervised to make any such movement successful.[17] Reno and Benteen, in their testimony, attempted to create the illusion that they were "driven back" from Weir Point to Reno hill by the overwhelming Indian forces. Recorder Lee did manage to extract enough of the facts from others to indicate that this was not true, and from Lieutenant Godfrey he received full proof. The troops were *ordered* back from Weir Point. No engagement took place there *until all but one troop had been withdrawn.* Godfrey, commanding that last troop to leave, was the only one to engage the Indians, in a valiant and successful effort to cover the retreat of his comrades, and by that time Custer and his men were dead.

As the last of the troopers with Custer, many searching frantically for one more cartridge, dropped silently to the dusty ground of Custer Hill, the tiny scrap of paper containing the last order ever to come from Custer — "Benteen, Come on — big village — be quick — bring packs —" still nestled unheeded in the pocket of the man to whom it had been addressed.

Three days later, after Generals Terry and Gibbon relieved the survivors and the identification of the dead bodies began, Captain Benteen stood over the naked corpse of General Custer and was heard to remark, "There he is, God damn him, he will never fight anymore."[18]

To the "overgrown drummer boy" it was a job well done, and he seemed to draw elation from the part he had played in bringing it about.

The Lion was dead.

SECTION III
The Case of the Perfidious Petition

Much of the testimony taken at the Reno Court of Inquiry was not, as tradition demands, "the whole truth and nothing but the truth." Especially is this true of statements made under oath by Captain Benteen, Major Reno and a select group of subordinate officers who felt some inexplicable compulsion either to change their testimony or to phrase it in such a manner as to cast a different implication on Reno's various actions. And the verbal testimony of the witnesses was not alone in this respect.

On the 24th day of the Inquiry, February 8, 1879, at 10:30 in the morning, Major Reno introduced as exhibits for the defense three related documents for the consideration of the Court. We find in the Official Transcript of the proceedings: "Major Reno then offered and read in evidence certain pages, copies of which are hereto appended and marked respectively Exhibits No. 9, No. 10, and No. 11."

Exhibit No. 9 was a letter to Major Reno from the Adjutant General, E.D. Townsend. It read as follows:

Headquarters of the Army,
Adjutant General's Office,
Washington, August 10, 1876.

Major M.A. Reno
   7th Cavalry
(Through Headquarters Military Division of the Missouri)
Sir:
   Referring to the petition of the enlisted men of the 7th
Cavalry (forwarded by you the 15th ultimo) for the promotion
of yourself and other officers of the regiment who participated in
the engagement of June 25, 1876, I have the honor to enclose
herewith, for the information of the officers and enlisted men
concerned, a copy of the remarks of the General of the Army
with reference to the request contained in the petition.

Very Respectfully,
Your obedient Servant,
(signed) E.D. TOWNSEND,
Adjutant General

   As may be asssumed from the wording of the letter,
Major Reno, as acting commander of the 7th Cavalry, had
forwarded a petition through channels written by the
enlisted men of his command which pleaded for his
promotion as well as the promotion of other officers of the
regiment. In view of Major Reno's record at the Little Big
Horn, as developed in the previous chapters, the very
existence of such a document lauding the conduct of Reno
becomes most provocative. Exhibit No. 10, introduced at
the Court of Inquiry, turned out to be a copy of that
petition. Here, in full, is Exhibit No. 10:

Camp Near Big Horn on
Yellowstone River,
July 4, 1876

To his
Excellency the President
   and the Honorable Representatives
     of the United States.
Gentlemen:
   We the enlisted men, the survivors of the battle on the

Heights of Little Horn River, on the 25th and 26th of June, 1876, of the 7th Regiment of Cavalry who subscribe our names to this petition, most earnestly solicit the President and Representatives of our Country, that the vacancies among the Commissioned officers of our Regiment, made by the slaughter of our brave, heroic, now lamented Lieutenant Colonel George A. Custer, and the other noble dead Commissioned officers of our Regiment who fell close by him on the bloody field, daring the savage demons to the last, be filled by the Officers of the Regiment only. That Major M.A. Reno, be our Lieutenant Colonel vice Custer, killed; Captain F.W. Benteen our Major vice Reno, promoted. The other vacancies to be filled by officers of the Regiment by seniority. *Your petitioners know this to be contrary to the established rule of promotion,* but prayerfully solicit a deviation from the usual rule in this case, as it will be conferring a bravely fought for and justly merited promotion on officers who by their bravery, coolness and decision on the 25th and 26th of June 1876, saved the lives of every man now living of the 7th Cavalry who participated in the battle, one of the most bloody on record and one that would have ended with the loss of life of every officer and enlisted man on the field only for the position taken by Major Reno, which he held with bitter tenacity against fearful odds to the last. (italics mine, C.dB.)

To support this assertion — had our position been taken 100 yards back from the brink of the heights overlooking the river we would have been entirely cut off from water; and from behind those heights the Indian demons would have swarmed in hundreds picking off our men by detail, and before midday June 26th not an officer or enlisted man of our Regiment could have been left to tell of our dreadful fate as we then would have been completely surrounded.

With prayerful hope that our petitions be granted, we have the honor to forward it through our Commanding Officer.

Very Respectfully,

The 237 signatures which followed were not included as part of Exhibit No. 10. This petition, as orginally sent, never

1 Aug 21 George H. Drury &c
2   George W. Pease
3   Henry W B Medlin
4   Timothy Daley
5   Ener Neison
6   Thos Sawhorne
7   James Kelly
8   Wm O'Regan
9   John Hunt
10   Chas Windolph
11   James McNamara
12   Chas Fisher
13   Aloyes Diethoven
14   H J Kief

ENLISTED MEN'S PETITION

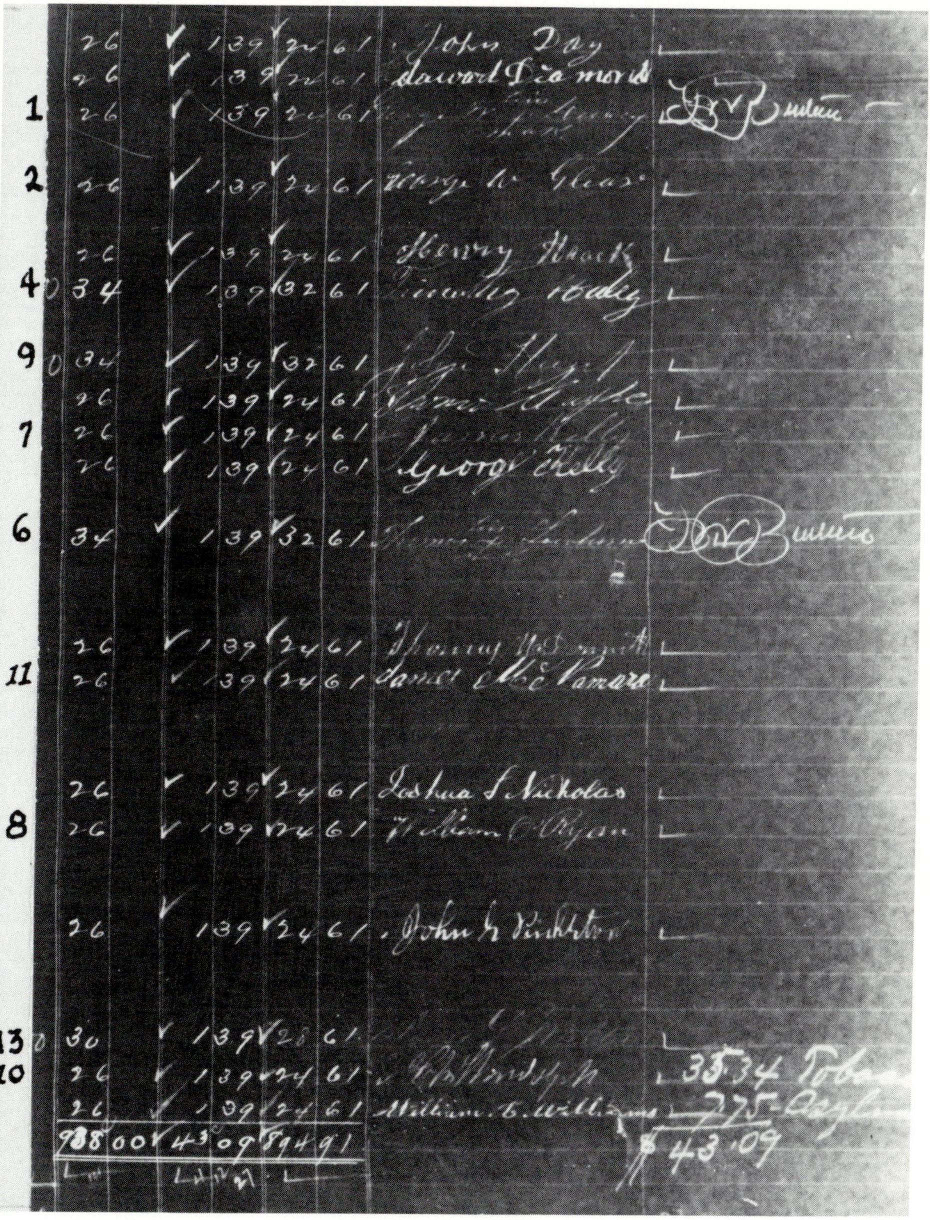

Payroll

reached the President, Ulysses S. Grant, nor "the Honorable Representatives of the United States." However, it did go as far as the General of the Army, William Tecumseh Sherman, who replied to the petitioners in the following letter, admitted into the Record of the Court of Inquiry as Exhibit No. 11:

> Headquarters Army of the United
> States, Washington, D.C.
> August 5, 1876.

The judicious and skilful conduct of Major Reno and Captain Benteen is appreciated, but the promotions caused by General Custer's death have been made by the President and confirmed by the Senate; therefore this petition cannot be granted. When the Sioux campaign is over I shall be most happy to recognize the valuable services of both officers and men by granting favors or recommending actual promotion.

Promotion on the field of battle was Napoleon's favorite method of stimulating his officers and soldiers to deeds of heroism, but it is impossible in our service because commissions can only be granted by the President on the advice and consent of the Senate, and except in original vacancies, promotion in a regiment is generally if not always made on the rule of seniority.

> W.T. Sherman
> General

In this manner the "Enlisted Men's Petition" and the attendant correspondence acknowledging it was made a part of the Official Record of the Court of Inquiry. Was the petition instrumental in clearing the name of Major Reno? Reno's counsel, Lyman D. Gilbert, certainly was aware of its implications on behalf of his client. In his concluding remarks to the Court, summarizing the defense of Major Reno, Gilbert managed to make reference to the document, a pointed reference that was most probably recalled by the Court in preparing the verdict. Gilbert said, with considerable flourish, 'Aye, even the privates and non-commissioned officers, on what was almost the field of battle, with one voice commend him and his brother officers for promotion for soldierly bearing — *and the General of the Army received with approbation their high praise of his conduct.*'' (Italics mine, C.dB.)

For three-quarters of a century this document has been a source of frustration for those who have searched for the truth about Reno's conduct at the Little Big Horn. No matter what facts were discovered to Reno's discredit, this apparently unimpeachable testimonial to Reno by the men who served under him seemed to be irrefutable. Whenever a statement critical of Reno was made, his defenders would reply to the effect, "Well, here's what the enlisted men thought of him!" Perhaps it was for this reason that historians began to doubt. In later years survivors were questioned about the petition.[1] None of them remembered any such document being circulated among the men, and when confronted with the information that they had supposedly signed the document, merely shrugged and commented to the effect, "I've signed so many papers in the army, I might have signed this one. If you say that I did, you may be right, but I don't remember it."

Strange, isn't it? None of the men questioned recalled such an important document! Can this be blamed on faulty memory? Perhaps in part. Or could the petition be a fraud perpetrated by the "villains in the piece" as they cast lots for the dead Custer's epaulets?

It was not until the early 1950s that the curiosity, if you will, of the then Superintendent of Custer Battlefield National Monument, the late Major Edward S. Luce, inspired him to submit a photostatic copy of the signatures on the petition, together with a photostatic copy of a payroll of the 7th Cavalry for comparison of handwriting to determine the authenticity of the petition. The material was presented to the Federal Bureau of Investigation, Washington, D.C., an impartial organization, yet one whose official investigative conclusions were beyond question. The report of the FBI, now a matter of public record at Custer Battlefield Museum, had some rather startling facts to disclose. Submitted for examination were photostatic copies of: the Enlisted Men's Petition, a copy of a letter dated August 10, 1876, in the known handwriting of E.D. Townsend (quoted above as Exhibit No. 9), a Muster Roll of the Field, Staff and Band of the 7th Cavalry, showing known signatures of members of this unit, and Muster Rolls of Headquarters Detachment and the 12 companies of the regiment, all bearing the known signature of members of these units. The Petition was designated by the Bureau as "Qc1" and other submissions as "Kc1" through "Kc15." (The complete report will be found in the appendix of this book, under the signature of J. Edgar Hoover, Director, dated November 2, 1954).

Let us examine this report, beginning with the material immediately following the heading, "Result of examination:"

> The signatures on the petition previously submitted ... have been compared with the respective signatures on specimens Kc1 through Kc15, but because of the limited amount of comparable known handwriting and the fact the the original specimens are not available, a definite conclusion could not be reached regarding these questioned signatures. *However, variations were noted in the signatures listed below and the corresponding known signatures which suggest in all probabilty that the signatures on the petition are forgeries.*

The "signatures listed below" included the names of 79 members of the 7th Cavalry Regiment. Major Luce, in his examination of the document in question, had noted that many of the signatures were written in handwriting that strongly resembled that of Joseph McCurry, first sergeant of Company H. Major Luce requested the FBI to ascertain if Sergeant McCurry had forged the majority of the signatures, and if not, who had done so. The Bureau reported:

> It could not *definitely* be determined whether or not Joseph

McCurry prepared any of the above-listed signatures [i.e., the first 79] because of the limited amount of comparable known handwriting of McCurry available.(All italics in this section are mine. C.dB.)

Yet the use of the word "definitely" suggests that even the FBI may have suspected McCurry, but without more evidence they could not commit themselves.

The report concluded with: "There is insufficient comparable known handwriting of any individual in the known specimens to determine whether or not any of these individuals wrote the petition . . ."

We have, then, 79 of 237 signatures to the petition labeled by the FBI as "probable forgeries," and the official opinion that, due to a lack of additional handwriting specimens, the identity of the forger and the identity of the author of the petition (possibly the same individual) could not be definitely established. What then of the remaining signatures? The FBI reports continues:

"There are listed below the names of the individuals whose names appeared on the petition *but who signed the payroll with a witnessed 'x'.* " (Italics mine, C.dB.)

Here 17 men were named who regularly signed their company payrolls with an "x," witnessed by an officer, yet these same men signed their names to the Enlisted Men's Petition with excellent penmanship! To demonstrate more graphically the incredible audacity of the person responsible for forging the names of men who could not even write, a photostatic excerpt showing a partial list of the "signers" from one page of the petition is reproduced following page 49.

For ease of comparison the list of names have been numbered at the left. Corresponding numbers to identify the same signatures are found on the excerpt of the payroll which is reproduced following page 49.

It will be noted that two discrepancies appear instantly in

comparing these two photostats. Numbers 1 and 6, "George W. Dewey" and "Thomas Lawhorn," inscribed with skillful penmanship on the petition, are represented by an "x" on the payroll, with the words "his mark" written above and below the "x" and the man's name carefully spelled out either by the company clerk or the witnessing officer who was always the company commander. The name of the officer appears in the extreme right column, "F.W. Benteen." Yet these are but two of the 17 men listed by the FBI in their report, gleaned from both the entire signatures on the petition and the entire muster rolls of the regiment. The reader is invited to compare the two photostats reproduced. There are other names (numbered correspondingly by the author) appearing on both documents, but which do not appear reasonably similar. Compare the No. 4 signature, "Timothy Haley." Note the variations in the formations of the capital letter "H" and in the small letter "y" which appears twice in the same name. On the petition the "y" is brought straight down. On the payroll, both "y's" are looped. It should be obvious even to the unpracticed eye that the petition signatures of Haley and James Kelly (Nos. 4 and 7) were written by one man, and that the same forger wrote the name of "John Hunt" (No. 9). Note the similarity in the formation of the capital "H" in both "Haley" and "Hunt." The capital letter "J" in No. 9, John Hunt, is identical with the "J" in No. 7, James Kelly, and both names slant to the right. Unfortunately there are no other letters common to both names for further examination.

The name of "Aloyes L. Walter" (No. 13) appears so faintly on the payroll that it is difficult to use it in comparison with the petition signature. However one glaring discrepancy does appear. On the petition the name appears as "Walters" and it defintely known to be "Walter." Surely Walter know how to spell his own name! Compare the first names of Charles Windolph and Charles Fisher (Nos. 10 and 12). Both signatures on the petition show the abbreviation "Chas.," and on examination appear to be exact duplicates in every detail. Charles Windolph, the last survivor of the Battle of the Little Big Horn, was one of those who failed to recall any knowledge of the petition and who denied having signed it. The name of No. 8, William O'Ryan, on the payroll bears little resemblance to the name on the petition. The names of Haley, Hunt, Kelly, Walter, Windolph, and O'Ryan all appear on the list of 79 probable forgeries. Only the name of Charles Fisher is missing from that list, but a comparison of his two "signatures" would suggest that he was also a victim of forgery. The FBI report listed an additional eight signatures for which "no known signatures could be located in the specimens for comparison." The name of Charles Fisher is included in that list, and Company designation, H, makes his presence at the time the petition was signed suspect. There were two Charles Fishers with the regiment: one was a Trumpeter with Company M, and the other was a private with K Company. This latter man was transferred to Company H on July 1, but was not present with the regiment at that time, being on duty at the Powder River supply depot, about 150 miles away!

Nor was Fisher the only one. An examination of the regiment's Roster of Survivors, dated June 30, 1876, discloses the names of a number of men who were on detached service at the Powder River base. None of these men were present at the Battle of the Little Big Horn, nor were they present in the camp at the mouth of the Big Horn on July 4, the place and date marking the "birth" of the Enlisted Men's petition. Obviously none of these men on detached service could have signed the petition, yet we find the signatures of three men who were on duty at Powder River. These men were Privates Aloyes Walter (mentioned previously), Charles H. Houghtaling and Walter Sterland. The names of all three appear in the list of 79 signatures that the Federal Bureau of Investigation considered, "in all probability ... are forgeries." More to the point, they are all *definite* forgeries.

A careful examination of the roster of survivors fails to disclose the names of two alleged signers of the petition, nor are they accounted for among the dead, wounded, missing, detached, deserted or on military leave. In short, the names of Privates William H. Shields and Lori Marbrey are not included on any regimental record of that day, yet their "signatures", appear on the Enlisted Men's petition of July 4. We do not pretend to possess an explanation for this irregularity and must assume that the names were either invented by the forger (or forgers) of the petition or were merely overlooked by an incompetent company clerk. The latter explanation is weakened by the fact that the names of the men do not appear on the payroll for June and it is difficult to believe that the poorly paid enlisted men of our frontier army would accept this oversight without a protest. Had a protest been made, a correction would have assuredly been made on the rosters of the regiment and the two would have been accounted for today. The absence of the names of Shield and Marbrey from regimental records places their signatures on the petition under suspicion of forgery.[2]

Why would anyone perpetrate such a hoax as this? The answer is not difficult to find. Both Reno and Benteen had good reason to feel that such a testimonial of faith and devotion would serve their causes well should they ever be called upon to account for their actions during the battle. A well-placed word with a reliable "go between" from the enlisted ranks might well be the only step necessary to place the wheels in motion. The selection of the "right" man for the job might involve some conniving, and a close relationship based on previous association would be necessary to insure that the man selected could be trusted. What enlisted man enjoys a position that allows for easy access to both officers and the enlisted ranks? To a large degree the first sergeant of a company fills the qualifications more than any other one man in a military organization. To be sure the sergeant-major would be even more suited to the task, but the regimental sergeant-major had died with Custer and no one had as yet been appointed to that role. Major Reno was a field officer not commanding a company and would not enjoy a close relationship with any enlisted man. Eliminating Reno we have Captain Benteen, commanding officer of Company H. Is it not odd that the very man suspected of the forgeries was none other than Joseph McCurry, Benteen's first sergeant?

In the original petition the author of it acknowledged that such a request was "contrary to the established rule of promotion." He was substantiated in this belief by the General of the Army, William T. Sherman, who in his reply states, "Promotion of the field of battle ... is impossible in our service." Why, then, should the petitioners, in full knowledge that the petition would be denied, proceed to file it? The answer is this: the purpose of the petition was not to plead for the promotion of Reno and Benteen, but for the exoneration of Reno and Benteen. It was intended only to bring to the attention of General Sherman and the President, as well as any and all others in authority who might read it, the fact that the enlisted men of the command, in a position to observe firsthand the conduct of Reno and Benteen, found them to be above reproach, and that their "bravery, coolness and decision on the 25th and 26th of June 1876, saved the lives of every man now living of the 7th Cavalry who participated in the battle ..." On July 4, 1876, nine days after the battle ended, Reno and Benteen were certainly above suspicion, at least as far as the general public and the top ranking Army officials were concerned. But no one knew more fully than they that an investigation of their conduct would bring to light, eventually, a more accurate picture of their activities during the engagement. Only an enormous sense of guilt could compel Reno and Benteen to attempt to pre-arrange the evidence in advance of any possible inquiry, and a complete vindication by the enlisted men would weigh heavily in any decision that might be made later.

The reader must bear in mind that these allegations are hypothetical even though they have basis in reason. Let us review the evidence as it has been developed:

(1) The actions of Reno and Benteen at the Battle of the Little Big Horn were such as to insure the failure of the mission. The complete lack of cooperation with the specific orders of the commanding officer, the lack of confidence in him, the open hostility they held for him and the insubordination of the battalion commanders could result in nothing but a negative conclusion to the mission.

(2) The loss of the engagement to the Indians, the loss of five troops of the regiment including the commanding officer himself, a man nationally famed for his abilities in battle, could not be written off either by the War Department or the American people as merely one of the unfortunate but inevitable tragedies of war. Of this Reno and Benteen were well aware.

(3) In the full knowledge that they would be called upon to account for the catastrophe in a manner fully acceptable to all, there was a great need for "fence mending" in advance of such an inquiry.

(4) A testimonial, freely given by the enlisted men of the command would stand as vindication beyond reproach in the eyes of any who might question the battalion commanders.

(5) An officer could not circulate a petition in his own behalf, especially one purporting to be the unsolicited appreciation of subordinates for that officer's heroism, and a request that he be promoted in rank on the basis of that heroism.

(6) Such a petition could be promulgated by an intermediary, providing one could be found who filled the

necessary qualifications of complete trust and reliability together with the advantage of free association with enlisted men and officers alike.

(7) The ideal intermediary would be the first sergeant of a company; necessarily one completely dominated by the officer, and one whose loyalty and willingness to serve in such a *sub rosa* role was assured.

(8) The first sergeant required for the task must be assigned to the command of the officer seeking the favor. Inasmuch as Reno was not in command of a company and Benteen was, the obvious choice would be Joseph McCurry, first sergeant of Company H, whose handwriting bears a strong similarity to a number of the signatures on the petition.

(9) Add to all this the incontestable result of the examination by the Federal Bureau of Investigation that " ...in all probability ...the signatures on the petition are forgeries." Bear in mind that this conclusion of the FBI, conservative as it is, was based on meager handwriting samples. Remember also your own observations of the handwriting comparisons in the accompanying photostats.

Who wrote the petition? It really doesn't matter. Who perpetrated the fraud? To answer that we need only ask a further question: who had the most to gain from it? Only Reno and Benteen qualify, and a study of the literary ability and florid style of Captain Benteen singles him out for the full responsibility. Certainly Benteen was clever enough to execute the document, assuredly he was in a position to carry it through, and above all, he, more than anyone else, realized the importance — indeed the necessity of such a testimonial. It is unfortunate that seventy-five years passed before the truth regarding the Enlisted Men's Petition was brought to light, it is equally unfortunate that the petition was allowed in evidence at the Reno Court of Inquiry. Perhaps a verdict more concordant with the facts might have resulted.

BVT. MAJOR GENERAL GEORGE A. CUSTER
From the Elizabeth B. Custer Collection
Courtesy of Custer Battlefield National Monument

SECTION IV
The Case Against General Custer

To summarize with any degree of effectiveness the events which resulted in the Battle of the Little Big Horn, it is necessary to examine the part played in that great drama by the regiment's lieutenant-colonel and commanding officer, Brevet Major General George Armstrong Custer. A brief of evidence purporting to lay the blame for that disaster at the feet of Major Reno and Captain Benteen must be accompanied by a strict accounting of the actions of Custer, either to exonerate him of any deliberate action leading to the defeat of the regiment or to accuse him of complicity in bringing about that defeat by his own performance.

General Custer is accused on two counts: (1) Deliberate disobedience of General Terry's orders, and (2) Inexpedient tactics employed in the battle itself.[1]

The first indictment is based upon the written instructions issued by the commander of the expedition, Brevet Major General Alfred Terry, through his acting assistant adjutant general, Captain E.W. Smith of the 18th Infantry. These Instructions were the direct result of a conference between Custer, Terry and Brevet Major General John Gibbon, commander of the Montana column, aboard the supply steamer, "Far West," at the mouth of the Rosebud River on June 21, the day before Custer marched with his regiment to the

Little Big Horn. The contents of the written order represented a summary of mutual agreement between the officers concerned regarding the successful prosecution of the hostiles based upon the information available at the time. The order opened with these words:

"The Brigadier-General Commanding directs that as soon as your regiment can be made ready for the march, you will proceed up the Rosebud in pursuit of the Indians whose trail was discovered by Major Reno a few days since."

There can be no doubt that this was a direct order. Accordingly, the 7th Cavalry left the mouth of the Rosebud at noon, June 22, following the Rosebud in complete compliance with Terry's directive.

The order continued: 'It is, of course, impossible to give you any definite instructions in regard to this movement, and were it not impossible to do so the Department Commander places too much confidence in your zeal, energy, and ability to wish to impose upon you precise orders which might hamper your actions when nearly in contact with the enemy."[2]

The full import of these words cannot be overstressed, for it is an admission of the Expedition Commander that no one knew at that time exactly where Custer was to go, what he would find or how he would find it. The Rosebud-Little Big Horn country was almost entirely unknown.[3] The map used in tracing the suggested movements of the forces in the field during the previous night's conference represented the courses of the streams south of the Yellowstone by dotted lines; the terrain of the area was hardly represented at all. A comparison between this early map and the detail of a modern map of the region shows obvious discrepancies in distance, detail and location. As Terry admitted, "It is, of course, impossible to give you any definite instruction ..." The burden of responsibility of Custer's pursuit of the hostiles was his alone. In the face of later recriminations against Custer, it is well to recall Terry's words of praise, "...the Department Commander places too much confidence in your zeal, energy, and ability ..." Custer's orders continued:

"He [Terry] will, however, indicate to you his own views of what your action should be, and he desires that you should conform to them *unless you shall see sufficent reason for departing from them.'* [4] (Italics mine, C.dB.)

The order then outlines Terry's "views:" "He thinks that you should proceed up the Rosebud until you ascertain definitely the direction of which the trail above spoken of leads. Should it be found (as it appears almost certain that it will be found) to turn towards the Little Horn,[5] he thinks that you should still proceed southward, perhaps as far as the headwaters of the Tongue, and then turn towards the Little Horn, feeling constantly, however, to your left, so as to preclude the possibility of the escape of the Indians to the south or southeast by passing around your left flank."

How did Terry, Gibbon and Custer predict the location of the Indians so precisely? Certainly not from studying their map! Only someone very familiar with the area could have given them the information which enabled them to pinpoint the route the Indians would follow, and that someone could only be Michel "Mitch" Bouyer, the half-Sioux, half-French scout with the Crow Indian detachment.

The eastern boundary of the Crow Reservation, as defined by the Treaty of 1868, follows the upper reaches of the Rosebud River. Bouyer, Thomas LeForge and the Crow Indians employed as scouts knew this area intimately. Although Bouyer, or any others with the Crow detachment, are not mentioned as being present at the conference aboard the "Far West," it would be unreasonable to believe they were not present to advise the army on the nature of the terrain into which they would soon enter.

The Crows knew very well that the hostile trail on the

Rosebud would be heading for what was known as "Indian Paradise," and by following that stream to its headwaters, they would find themselves just over the divide of the Wolf mountains and a short distance from their destination. This area was noted for its many streams and excellent forage. It abounded in deer, buffalo and other game on which the Indians depended for food.

Returning to Terry's orders:

> The column of Colonel Gibbon is now in motion for the mouth of the Big Horn. As soon as it reaches that point it will cross the Yellowstone and move up at least as far as the Big and Little Horns. Of course its future movements must be controlled by circumstances as they arise, but it is hoped that the Indians, if upon the Little Horn, may be so nearly inclosed by the two columns that their escape will be impossible.

To assist the reader in following the overall strategy of to this we need only refer to the map on page xvi. Obviously Little Big Horn River on the left, and the Rosebud River on the right, both flowing in a general northerly direction. It will be noted that the Rosebud turns abruptly west at "B," designated as the Big Bend," and rises in the southern portion of the Wolf Mountains only a few miles distant. There are a number of passes in this area providing easy access to the Little Big Horn valley and to some of the streams that are tributaries of the Little Big Horn River (the area encircled on bottom left of the map). This is the area known as "Indian Paradise."

With this in mind Terry's orders make sense: that "should it be found (as appears almost certain that it will be found) to turn toward the Little Horn, he thinks that you [Custer] should still proceed southward, perhaps as far as the headwaters of the Tongue, and then towards the Little Horn, feeling constantly, however, to your left, so as to preclude the possibility of the escape of the Indians to the south or southeast . . ."

Such a maneuver would place Custer to the southeast of

"Indian Paradise" and would cut off their retreat when Gibbon's men pushed toward them from the north. It was a cleverly devised scheme and should have been successful if other circumstances had not intervened.

A Cheyenne hunting party discovered the troops of General George Crook approaching the upper reaches of the Rosebud on June 8. Returning to the main body of the hostiles, they found them encamped at the mouth of Davis Creek (Number "1" on the map). The Indians realized that their route to "Indian Paradise" was now closed to them, and they turned to the west, following Davis Creek, and then down to the forks of a stream known as Reno Creek where they made camp. (Number "3" on the map.).

General Crook reached the South Fork of the Rosebud on June 16 ("A" on the map) and the following morning moved along that stream to a position just west of "Big Bend"("B" on the map), where they stopped for breakfast and to rest the horses and men. During this halt, on June 17, the command was attacked by a large force of warriors from the camp on Reno Creek and the resulting "Battle of the Rosebud" raged until mid-afternoon. When the Indians broke off the engagement and returned to the main camp, Crook withdrew to his base on Goose Creek, the site of present-day Sheridan, Wyoming.[6]

The discovery of Crook's troops on the Rosebud was the unforeseen circumstances that nullified Terry's orders. If the had not happened the Indians would have continued south, then west along the Rosebud as they intended to do, and Custer would have followed them in full compliance with his orders. But Crook had blocked the Indian's intended route, forcing them to leave the Rosebud 20 miles north of the "Big Bend." Custer, whose orders were to pursue the Indians, had no choice but to follow them.

It must be remembered that Terry's strategy, as outlined in his orders to Custer, is the only plan of operation that exists. In

Terry's first report to General Sheridan after Custer's defeat, dated June 27, he mentioned no plan and attached no blame for the disaster. Yet in his second report, dated July 2, a week after the battle, Terry outlined a more detailed strategy, adding that " . . . our plan must have been successful had it been carried out . . ." It would appear that "fence-mending" in advance of a later inquiry was not confined to the lower ranks! The only plan was that which was found in Custer's orders, and though it was understandably vague and indefinite it was never-the-less a plan.

Custer's orders continued:

> The Department Commander desires that on your way up the Rosebud you should thoroughly examine the upper part of Tullock's Creek, and that you should endeavor to send a scout through to Colonel Gibbon's column with information of the result of your examination. The lower part of this creek will be examined by a detachment from Colonel Gibbon's command.

It is alleged that Custer definitely and deliberately defied Terry's authority by his failure to comply with this portion of his instructions. It is said that Custer did not "thoroughly examine the upper part of Tullock's Creek," and that he did not "send a scout through to Colonel Gibbon's column with information of the result" of that examination. For the answer General Terry the map on page xvi is provided. It shows the Terry was under the impression that Custer would pass through this area in the normal course of his pursuit. It was a physical impossibility for Custer to scout the Tullock and still follow his instructions to "proceed up the Rosebud in pursuit of the Indians" as this would require a turning due west instead of proceeding south. It would have been possible to send a scout to the Tullock and then on to the Gibbon column, but this would have been of no benefit to anyone. As later developments proved, the Indians were not on Tullock's Creek and the scouts would have accomplished nothing. However later developments do not serve as an excuse for disobedience. General Gibbon had assigned one of his scouts, George Herendeen, to accompany Custer and act as the scout to be sent back with the information gathered as a result of the examination of Tullock's Creek. One of Custer's early critics, Major James Brisbin who commanded the cavalry under Gibbon, was particularly vehement in condemning Custer for his failure to make use of Herendeen's services in this respect, and in a letter to Lieutenant Godfrey, dated January 1892, he stated:

> Herendeen was to come down the Tullock [sic] and communicate with Gibbon or Terry or myself when your column crossed that stream or channel." (Note that Brisbin, too, expected that Tullock was actually on Custer's line of march). "Herendeen did report to Custer when you reached Tullock[7] and said, 'General , this is the Tullock, and here is where I am to leave you and go down it to the other command.' Custer was riding on his horse at the time and Herendeen rode up beside him. Custer gave Herendeen no answer, but heard him and looked at him. Herendeen kept near the general for some time, expecting to be called and dispatched down the Tullock to us; but seeing he was not wanted he fell back and followed along. Nor did Custer ever speak to him again, though he knew Herendeen was there to go down the Tullock and communicate with us by Terry's orders, and in this Custer disobeyed distinctly the Department Commander's wishes and orders. He did not wish us to know where he was or what he was doing, for fear we would get some of the credit of the campaign.[8]

This statement, impressive as it is, does not coincide with statements made by others. Perhaps the best authority of what passed between Custer and Herendeen would be Herendeen himself. In January 1878, just two years after the battle, Herendeen wrote to the New York *Herald* this account of the incident:

> On the morning of the 24th we broke camp at 5 o'clock and continued following the trail up the stream. Soon after starting

Custer, who was in advance with Bouyer, called me to him and told me to get ready, he thought he would send me and Charley Reynolds[9] to the head of Tullock's Fork to take a look. I told the General it was not time yet, as we were traveling in the direction of the head of Tullock,[10] and I could only follow his trail. I called Bouyer, who was a little ahead back and asked him if I was not correct in my statement to the General, and he said, "Yes; further up on Rosebud we would come opposite a gap, and then we could cut across and strike the Tullock in about fifteen miles ride." Custer said, "All right; I could wait."

From this account it is obvious that the proposed examination of the headwaters of Tullock's Creek was foremost in Custer's mind, as it was Custer who called Herendeen to him, and not — as Brisbin claimed — that Herendeen came to Custer. Why then did Custer fail to send Herendeen to Tullock when the regiment reached the "gap?" No one knows for certain, but it is probable that the information Custer received only a few hours later either drove the thought from his mind, or made such action unnecessary, for the scouts by then discovered that the trail, instead of continuing south along the Rosebud, had turned to the west near the mouth of Davis Creek and were heading for the Little Big Horn!

As no trail had been found leading toward Tullock, it was obvious that no Indians were in that vicinity. There is another statement from an observer with Custer, one whose integrity was above reproach.[11] That man was Lieutenant Godfrey, commanding K Company. In Godfrey's account of the battle he stated, "We made many long halts, so as not to get ahead of the scouts, *who seemed to be doing their work thoroughly, giving special attention to the right, toward Tullock's Creek,* the valley of which was in general view from the divide. Once or twice signal smokes were reported in that direction, but *investigation did not confirm the reports."*

From this we may conclude that Custer was keeping Tullock's Creek under surveillance as he marched —

"thoroughly," Godfrey says — and the last phrase indicates that the area was "investigated" if not "examined" as Terry requested. Colonel Robert P. Hughes[12] shrugs off Godfrey's account with the words, "This is certainly an error." Inasmuch as Godfrey was a member of Custer's command and Hughes was not, the reader is invited to accept the account which he personally finds the most authoritative.

It might be well to recall Terry's own words regarding his orders: that he desired that Custer should conform to them unless he should "see sufficient reason for departing from them." Apparently Custer's realization that the Indian trail did not turn towards Tullock Creek but continued up the Rosebud was sufficient reason to depart from that part of his orders.

The orders from Terry continued with a brief bit of information: "The supply steamer will be pushed up the Big Horn as far as the forks if the river is found to be navigable for that distance, and the Department Commander, who will accompany the column of Colonel Gibbon, desires you to report to him there not later than the expectation of the time for which your troops are rationed, unless in the meantime you hear further orders."

It can be stated positively that Custer did not at any time receive "further orders" from Terry, so that phrase of the instruction can be dispensed with immediately. That leaves Custer with the order to report to General Terry not later than the time for which his troops were rationed. We have excellent authority to establish this point. Lieutenant Godfrey who was present as a troop commander at the time Custer gave the preparatory instruction to the regimental officers at the mouth of the Rosebud on June 21, recalled, "We were to transport," on our pack-mules, *fifteen days rations* . . . " After listing the rations in detail Godfrey mentioned that "General Custer recommended that some extra forage be carried on the pack-mules. In endeavoring to carry out this recommendation some troop commanders (Captain Moylan and myself) foresaw the difficulties and told the General that some of the mules would certainly break down, especially if the extra forage were packed. He replied in an unusually emphatic manner, 'Well, gentlemen, you may carry what supplies you please; you will be held responsible for your companies. The extra forage was only a suggestion, but this fact bear in mind, *we will follow the trail for fifteen days unless we catch them before that time expires,* no matter how far it may take us from our base of supplies; we may not see the supply steamer again.'''

Godfrey reported that Custer added, "You had better carry along an extra supply of salt; we may have to live on horsemeat before we get through." According to Godrey, the officers complied.[13] We find, then, that Custer's troops were rationed for fifteen days, which meant that Custer was to report to Terry not later than July 6 if he was to comply with his orders. As mentioned earlier, General Terry dispatched two official reports to General Sheridan, the first dated June 27, bearing no mention of a plan of action, and the second, dated July 2, outlining his plans for the campaign. In Terry's words, "While at the mouth of the Rosebud I submitted my plan to Genl. Gibbon and to General Custer. They approved it heartily." This statement in Terry's second report was followed by a general summary of the written orders to Custer as reviewed in this chapter. The report concluded with: "I send in another dispatch a copy of my written orders to Custer, but these were supplemented by the distinct understanding that Gibbon could not get to the Little Big Horn *before the evening of the 26th.*" The inference, of course, was that Custer was to have effected a junction with Gibbon on that date. No where in Custer's written instuctions is there any hint of such a plan. Had there been any agreement of this kind between the commanding officers, why was it not officially mentioned in those orders? It appears today that the creation of a definite date of rendezvous was originated *post facto* as a part of the general "cover up" that seems to have spread like an epidemic among the principals of the participating commands.

Unfortunately, this accusation appears aimed specifically at "the kindest and noblest-hearted" man that Colonel Hughes had "ever known," the Department Commander himself (and the brother-in-law of Hughes), General Alfred Terry. The word "unfortunately" is used sincerely for Terry was indeed a brave and capable officer, and a fair and just commander. Yet we are faced with Terry's own statement that "Gibbon could not get to the Little Big Horn before the evening of the 26th." We could accept the statement at its face value without reading into it any inference, that all he wished to convey was the information that Gibbon would arrive on the 26th, if it were not for the repeated efforts of Colonel Hughes to prove that Terry very definitely had in mind a junction of Gibbon and Custer on that date. But it is simple to hoist Hughes "on his own petard" and let him convict himself of "erroneous reasoning," to employ a term less harsh than the deed deserved.

In his article, "Campaign Against the Sioux," Hughes stated: "It is well understood that Gibbon could not get in place without resorting to forced marches, before the 26th at the earliest, and also well understood that *if Custer marched as directed he would, at the same time, be where it was intended he should be, 'in cooperating distance,'* on the only possible line of retreat if the Indians should run away, while if they held their ground and fought *he would be able to make his attack a joint one with Gibbon."*

The absurdity of this statement will be developed later. First, let us give Colonel Hughes more "rope" so that he can do a more thorough job of hanging himself. He continues: "Custer made a forced march and held to the Indian trail instead of moving still southward, and this brought him on the night of the 24th into the position he ought to have occupied on the morning of the 26th, and at least twenty-four hours before Gibbon could possibly be expected to be in place."[14]

According to Hughes, if Custer had marched as directed he would have found himself where he belonged. And where was that? Also according to Hughes (and Custer's orders) "perhaps as far as the headwaters of the Tongue." Hughes stressed this point in his article: "Custer was left in no doubt what Terry intended he should do, and with no discretion to do otherwise than as ordered — 'still proceed southward, perhaps as far as the headwaters of the Tongue.'"

Custer's primary order was to pursue the Indians. The route he followed was that which Terry *believed* they would take. Once the Indians abandoned that route twenty miles north of the point where Terry expected them to "turn toward the Little Horn," that portion of the orders no longer applied. But the *primary* order was to pursue the Indians and Custer was required to do just that. Had he failed to do so and gone off on a "wild goose chase" to the headwaters of the Tongue, he would have been court-martialed. Yet Hughes insists that Custer should have arrived at the position he reached on the 24th two days later — on the 26!

The colonel raises the objection that Custer made forced marches to strike the Indians before Gibbon could possibly get in position, and in this Major Brisbin concurs. As Gibbon's chief of cavalry, Brisbin was understandably anxious to participate in the contemplated actions, although his anxiety is poor excuse for his vitriolic attack on the dead Custer. Brisbin wrote a letter to Lieutenant Godfrey that Custer ". . . did not wish us to know where he was or what he was doing, for fear we would get some of the credit of the campaign. Custer was jealous of Gibbon . . ." And again, Brisbin claimed that Custer remarked to a fellow officer, "This is to be a 7th Cavalry battle, and I want all the glory for the 7th Calvalry there is in it."

Brisbin, in a schoolboy rage, commented, "The insufferable

ass got it!", and in the same letter he refers to Custer as a ". . . wild man [turned] loose with the lives of 650 precious men in his hands."[15]

As for the alleged "forced march" up the Rosebud, General Nelson A. Miles commented, "The fact of his slow marches indicates his care and judiciousness in going from the mouth of the Rosebud to the battlefield on the Little Big Horn. The first day's march was only four hours, or twelve miles in distance. The second day, June 23, thirty-three miles or twelve hours march, with long halts for the purpose of examining trails, abandoned camps, and evidence of the presence of Indians. The third day, the 24th, twelve hours march or twenty-eight miles. The night of the 24th, between 11:30 and the morning of the 25th, he moved ten miles in order to conceal his movement and position from the enemy. On the morning of the 25th, between eight and ten, he moved ten miles, later fifteen; in all, 108 miles in four days."[16]

Simple computation will reveal that Custer averaged only 27 miles per day. Compare this figure with the estimate Terry requested of Custer in planning the details of the campaign. At that time Custer estimated he would average *thirty miles per day*. Therefore Custer marched his regiment slower than he hoped he would do.

The best measurement of whether Custer's march up the Rosebud was forced would be the condition of the horses. The following statements were taken during the Reno Court of Inquiry in 1879:

Fred Gerard, civilian interpreter: "The horses of the command did not seem fatigued; they were on the bit; mine was; and comparatively fresh."

Dr Porter, acting assistant surgeon: "The horses were in good condition. High spirited — some wanted to run."

Sergeant Edward Davern, Reno's orderly: "The horses of the command were in tolerable good condition."

Lieutennt Edward S. Godfrey: "The general condition of the horses was good."

We have no evidence from other sources to contradict these statements. It would appear, therefore, that all but a few of the horses were in a relatively good condition, and that any charges of Custer making "forced marches" are false.[17]

To return to Hughes' contention that Custer and Gibbon were to act jointly in the Little Big Horn valley on a specified date, we may close the argument with this observation of Lieutenant Godfrey:

> It has been assumed by some writers that General Terry's command would be at the mouth of the Little Big Horn on June 26, and that General Custer knew of that — also by some that the two commands were to come together about that date at that place. General Terry's instructions do not say when his command would reach that point, and according to the instructions, General Custer was not necessarily expected there before the 5th or 6th of July, being rationed for fifteen days.
>
> It is an absurdity to think that two commands, of 700 and 400, separated by from fifty to one-hundred miles, could coordinate their movements in that open country and hold the Hostiles for a co-operative attack ... There could not have been any understanding as contended by some, that the two commands of Custer and Gibbon were to meet at or near the mouth of the Little Big Horn on June 26th.[18]

And who claims Custer was impetuous, risking all for the glory of a smashing victory for the 7th and himself? The petulant Brisbin, jealous of Custer's national reputation and position; the churlish Hughes, fearful that the taint of guilt might be attached to his beloved brother-in-law, General Terry; Reno and Benteen, incompetent and insubordinate, must surely be included, and possibly even General Terry himself, despite Hughes protestations. Any censure from Sherman, Sheridan and Grant was second-hand, inspired entirely by such information as Terry provided them, supplemented by the personal motivation of Terry's informants.

It has been specifically charged that Custer, upon finding the Indian trail leading from the Rosebud along Davis Creek deliberately attacked prematurely to gather the glory for himself.[19] Colonel Hughes was one of the first to implant this insinuation. In the Hughes article we find this tell-tale paragraph:

> Captain Wallace, 7th Calvalry, in his itinerary of the march states, in speaking of this same camp and time, 'General Custer detemined to cross the divide that night' (referring to the night of the 24th).[20]

Certainly such a bald statement by one of the officers present with the regiment at the time would indicate that Custer was indeed guilty of "glory hunting," but Hughes was indulging in one of the most heinous of literary devices, quoting Wallace out of context. Here is Wallace's actual statement, quoting in full:

> Custer determined to cross the divide that night, *conceal the command, the next day find out the locality of the village, and attack the next morning [the 26th] at daylight.*"

And this statement of Wallace is substantiated by both Lieutenants Godfrey and Edgerly. Godfrey said,

> At all events, our presence had been discovered and further concealment was unnecessary; that we would move at once to attack the village; and that *he [Custer] had not intended to make the attack until the next morning, the 26th,* but our discovery made it imperative to act at once, as delay would allow the village to scatter and escape.[21]

Edgerley's account is almost identical:

> The officers all went to where he [Custer] was, and he told us that our presence had been discovered; that his scouts had chased a small number of Indians that they had seen, and they had gotten away and gone in the direction of the Indian camp,

and as there was no use in trying to surprise them, *as his intentions had been, the next morning,* we would press on as quickly as we could and attack them in the village if possible.[22]

We come now to the question of whether the tactics employed by Custer in the battle preparations were sound or ill-considered. Were it not that Custer had been severely criticized for his strategy at the Little Big Horn it would be better to avoid any discussion of it. But Custer did not survive to defend himself. It is far too easy at this distance in time to become "an armchair quarterback" — to sit back and point out any mistake that might have been made, utilizing information we have today that Custer did not have on June 25, 1876. We must include in the list of such "second guessers" even some of those who participated in the action on that day, men who — after the battle and fully aware of the results — set themselves up as judges of the commanding officer's conduct, one of them going so far as to claim that he knew Custer's plan was wrong before the conflict began, but felt that he should keep his opinions to himself.[23] And again we are faced with the incontestable fact that had the regiment defeated the Indians instead of losing to them, these very same tactics would have been accepted as most judicious.[24]

Colonel Hughes refused to condemn Custer for the actual strategy he employed in the battle and so did Major Brisbin. Captain Benteen made only one specific charge: that Custer's division of the regiment alone was responsible for the tragedy, although he inferred on many occasions, that Custer's "impetuosity" as well as his "glory hunting" were contributory. Reno, of course, concurred in this opinion.

We have already shown that Custer had intended to rest his regiment in the Wolf Mountains for the day before attacking the Indians at daybreak, June 26. The discovery of his command by the hostiles destroyed the feasibility of this plan immediately.[26] There was no choice but to attack at once if Custer expected to hit the Indians at all, otherwise they would have time to scatter and escape in all directions.

At a point one mile west of the divide Custer divided the regiment into battalions, as previously reported, under Major Reno and Captain Benteen. Custer retained control of five companies[25] and Captain McDougall and his company were to acompany the pack-train. At the time Custer sent Benteen and his three companies to the southwest, he ordered the captain to "pitch into anything he might find." Custer had no firm information as to the exact location of the Indians. Had he possessed such knowledge it is doubtful that any division of the command would have been made at that time. It was believed that the hostiles were in the valley of the Little Big Horn, but were they spread out all along the river or were they in one camp? Custer's actions at the divide were comparable to an airplane pilot's flying by instrument, or as it is sometimes called, "flying blind." The fact that Benteen was detached to reconnoiter proves that Custer was not sure and that he was determined to pin-point the target before committing himself to action. Benteen was told that if he found nothing he was to report back to the main command. He was also instructed to "ride rapidly" in his search. This explains why Custer and Reno proceeded slowly down the creek, not wishing to be committed until word was received from Benteen. If Benteen found no Indians south of the line Custer and Reno were following, the command could be reunited and proceed in full force. There is no doubt that Benteen would have rejoined Custer and Reno had he moved at a faster pace, probably before the main column reached the Lone Tepee at the site of the abandoned village.

It was at this site that Custer received the erroneous information from Gerard that the Indians were "running like devils," and his "reconnaissance in force," aptly described by Dr. Charles H. Kuhlman in his book. "Legend Into History," was over. The information meant to Custer that the enemy had been sighted and according to Gerard, was in full flight. Immediately Custer ordered Reno to charge after them, knowing that a harassment from the rear would fully occupy the rear-guard of the hostiles as well as create confusion in the moving Indian column. Custer continued at a walk, still waiting for Benteen to come up. By now Custer knew that Benteen would have found nothing on his scout to the left and should, therefore, be close behind him. About a mile from the river Custer was met by his adjutant, Lieutenant W. W. Cooke, who had accompanied Reno to the river. Cooke reported that the Indians were not running away as Gerard had said earlier. Turning to the right, Custer ordered the gallop and with his battalion rode to the bluffs overlooking the river. Reno was already committed and there was no point in ordering him to withdraw for it was fatal to retreat from an opposing Indian force. Reno was safe as long as he did not falter, therefore the need of support was not urgent. Confidently expecting Reno to comply with his orders, Custer moved along the bluffs to a point just north and east of what was to be called Reno hill where he paused to observe the village and assess the situation.

Now the valley opened before him and for the first time, Custer saw the actual size of the Indian encampment. John Martini, Custer's orderly-trumpeter, later testified that the general was elated by what he saw — a few women, children and dogs. The logical conclusion was that the troops had surprised the village after all, as was indeed the case, despite the information he had received earlier. Turning to the troops, Custer shouted, 'We've caught them napping!'[27] With that he ordered the command to resume the march.

It is obvious that Custer continued north in an effort to find a place to descend to the river, then to strike the village from the flank.[28] But from the point of Reno's Crossing and extending north to Medicine Tail Coulee, a distance of four miles, there was an unbroken line of bluffs bordering the river, ninety to one hundred feet high, and nowhere in that line was there a place of descent to the valley that was adequate to accomodate such a large military unit.

A short distance north of Reno hill Custer, through his brother, Captain Tom Custer of Company C, ordered Sergeant Daniel Kanipe to deliver an oral message to McDougall to "bring the packs straight across country." Then, moving on, he paused again at the head of a ravine (Cedar Coulee) that emptied into Medicine Tail Coulee, a broad, dry creekbed that gave the troops access to the river. During this brief halt Custer sent his orderly-trumpeter, John Martini, back to Benteen with the famous written message, "Benteen. Come on. Big Village. Bring Packs." As Martini rode off the column marched down the ravine. A halt was made as the troops moved to the head of Medicine Tail, then the command moved to the high ridge that forms the northern rim of the coulee. This move to high ground was probably to place the troops in a more visible position, not only to Benteen, but also to the hostiles in the valley. Such a maneuver would surely intimidate the Indians in the north end of the Village and would probably take some of the pressure off Reno.

Here, the story as it is known, comes to an end. What took place later affecting Custer's command is theory, for there were no survivors.[29] We must assume that General Custer applied the same logic to his later actions as he did in issuing orders to the other battalions, logic that was necessarily concluded from personal observation and from the information available at the time. To state that this logic was faulty is to ignore the failure of the other battalion commanders to comply with their orders. As General Miles later observed, "No commanding officer can win victories with seven-twelfths of his command remaining out of the engagement when within the sound of his rifle-shots."[30]

The immediate charge voiced against Custer's later tactics is that he must have been wrong, otherwise his command would not have been wiped out. Again we might answer that if Custer had won the battle, these same tactics would have been considered correct. There is no evidence that Custer's defeat was the direct result of unsound strategy while actually engaged in combat with the enemy. The Indians who fought him on that lonely ridge have never claimed that the victory was an easy one. If blame must be attached to this tragedy, let it be placed where it belongs. Here, in the author's opinion, as developed in these pages are the true causes of Custer's defeat on the Little Big Horn:

(1) *The erroneous information as to the fighting strength of the enemy.* If we are to find a scapegoat for this grievous error, we must search higher up the echelon of responsibility than Generals Terry, Sheridan and Sherman. Terry, Commander of the Department of the Dakota, said, "Custer expressed the utmost confidence he had all the force he could need, and *I shared his confidence.*"[31] Sherman, the General of the Army, stated, "Up to the moment of Custer's defeat there was nothing, official or private to justify an officer to expect that any detachment would encounter more than five hundred or eight hundred warriors."[32]

(2) *The mis-information Custer received from his scouts to the effect that his command had been discovered by the enemy.* This information, given with apparent basis in fact at the time, left Custer no choice. If he did not attack immediately, the Indians would scatter and escape,[33] or would have time to organize themselves for defense, or an attack on Custer, just as they had done only eight days before against the large force under General Crook. Had they had the opportunity to attack Custer while his command was still in the rough, high country of the Wolf Mountains it is unlikely that any of the regiment would have survived, for cavalry cannot manuever in such country. By attacking first, as Custer did, he caught the Indians

completely off guard and without any organization. Only after the easy defeat of Reno's Battalion did the Indians cease to act as a demoralized group and begin to function as a resolute and tenacious aggressor. Again, for an authoritative military opinion of Custer's decision, we have the words of General Sherman: "...he [Custer] could do nothing but attack when he found himself in the presence of the Indians."[34] As for Reno's lack of initiative and its ultimate penalty, we have the testimony of the Indians whom he attacked, that if he had maintained an aggressive front, they could not have dislodged him.[35]

(3) *The failure of Reno and Benteen to comply with their orders.* A military victory is basically the result of teamwork — complete cooperation and adherence to orders by all members of the participating units. Custer could not operate on the assumption that Reno would not hold on at the upper end of the village, that he would instead retreat — that Benteen would not bring up the ammunition and join him. A commander in battle *must* assume that his orders will be carried out, for his plans are based entirely upon that assumption. That is as true today as it was in 1876.[36]

(4) *The expending of ammunition.* Each trooper carried one hundred rounds of carbine cartridges: fifty on his person and fifty in his saddlebags. In addition each man was armed with a forty-five caliber Colt revolver and eighteen rounds of ammunition for it. It is obvious that this small amount of ammunition would be expended in a short time, and with the failure of Benteen to "bring up the packs," the fate of the men with Custer was sealed.

There may have been other causes that contributed to the great tragedy that took place on the heights above the Little Big Horn River, Montana Territory, June 25, 1876, but whatever they might have been will never be known. However, on the basis of established fact as to the causes we now know to have been contributory, defeat was inevitable. Any additional errors that might have been made, and of which we are not aware today, could not have changed the outcome in any material way. That is the tragedy of the Little Big Horn.

APPENDIX

The report of the Enlisted Men's Petition
from the Federal Bureau of Investigation
Washington, D.C., November 2, 1954.

REPORT
of the

FEDERAL BUREAU OF INVESTIGATION
WASHINGTON D. C.

To:
National Park Service
U. S. Department of the Interior
Washington 25, D. C.

November 2, 1954

Attention: Mr. Hillory A. Tolson
Assistant Director

Re: HANDWRITING COMPARISON FOR
CUSTER BATTLEFIELD NATIONAL
MONUMENT
DEPARTMENT OF THE INTERIOR
WASHINGTON, D. C.

John Edgar Hoover, Director

YOUR FILE NO. H2215-T
FBI FILE NO. 95-38320
LAB. NO.   D-192503 DG

Examination requested by: Addressee

Reference: Letter 10/12/54

Examination requested: Document

Specimens:

Resubmission of Qc1.

Kc1 Photostat of a letter dated August 10, 1876, in the known
handwriting of E. D. TOWNSEND.
Kc2 Photostat of a Muster Roll of the Field, Staff and Band of
the 7th Cavalry showing known signatures of members of this
unit.
Kc3 Photostat of a Muster Roll of a Detachment of the 7th Cavalry
showing known signatures of members of this unit.

Photostats of Muster Rolls of 12 companies of the 7th Cavalry
bearing known signatures of members of each company as follows:

Kc4   Company A
Kc5   Company B
Kc6   Company C
Kc7   Company D
Kc8   Company E
Kc9   Company F
Kc10 Company G
Kc11 Company H
Kc12 Company I
Kc13 Company K
Kc14 Company L
Kc15 Company M

Page 1

Continued next page

Result of examination:

     The **signatures** on the petition previously submitted
and designated as Qc1 have been compared with the respective
signatures on specimens Kc1 through Kc15 but because of the
limited amount of comparable known handwriting and the fact that
the original specimens are not available a definite conclusion
could not be reached regarding these questioned signatures. However,
variations were noted in the signatures listed below and the
corresponding known signatures which suggest the probability
that the signatures on the petition are forgeries.

Henry Fehler	(Company A)
John T. Easley	(Company A)
David McVeigh	(Company A)
John Bringes	(Company A)
Stanislos Roy	(Company A)
Louis Baumgartner	(Company A)
John W. Franklin	(Company A)
Emil O. Jonsan	(Company A)
William D. Nugent	(Company A)
John M. Gilbert	(Company A)
Anton Siebelder	(Company A)
Samuel Johnson	(Company A)
Neil Bancroft	(Company A)
John Crump	(Company B)
Michael Crowe	(Company B)
John O'Neill	(Company B)
James Pym	(Company B)
Ansgarious Boren	(Company B)
Patrick Crowley	(Company B)
Hiram W. Sager	(Company B)
John Sweeny	(Company F)
Martin Mullin	(Company C)
Frank Burwald	(Company E)
Fredrick Schutte	(Company F)
Charles Bank	(Company L)
Thomas McLaughlin	(Company H)
Mathew Maroney	(Company H)
George Geiger	(Company H)
William Ramell	(Company H)
Edward Diamond	(Company H)
Henry Haack	(Company H)
William C. Williams	(Company H)

D-192503 DG   Continued next page
Page 2

Timothy Haley	(Company H)
James Kelly	(Company H)
William O'Ryan	(Company H)
John Hunt	(Company H)
Charles Windolph	(Company H)
James McNamara	(Company H)
Aloyse L. Walter	(Company H)
C. H. Welch	(Company D)
Charles H. Houghtaling	(Company D)
William Gibbs	(Company K)
John Foley	(Company K)
W. W. Lasley	(Company K)
William Whittlon	(Company K)
George B. Penwell	(Company K)
Charles Chesterwood	(Company K)
Henry W. Raichel	(Company K)
John Rafter	(Company K)
Joseph Brown	(Company K)
Thomas A. Gordon	(Company K)
Michael Murphy	(Company K)
Christian Schlafer	(Company K)
Alonzo Jennys	(Company K)
John Schwerer	(Company K)
John Donahue	(Company K)
George Heid	(Company M)
Jean B. D. Gallene	(Company M)
Charles Weidman	(Company M)
Morris Cain	(Company M)
Frank Stratton	(Company M)
Edward Pigford	(Company M)
Hugh N. Moore	(Company M)
Walter S. Sterland	(Company M)
Frank Sniffin	(Company M)
Levi Thornberry	(Company M)
Charles Kavanaugh	(Company M)
Bernard Golden	(Company M)
Daniel Mahoney	(Company M)
Andrew Fredrick	(Company K)
Christian Boissen	(Company K)
Cornelius Bresnahan	(Company K)
John Shauer	(Company K)
Charles Burkhardt	(Company K)
Wilson McConnell	(Company K)

Continued next page

Thomas Murphy	(Company K)
Martin McCue	(Company K)
August Siefart	(Company K)
John R. Steintker	(Company K)

It could not definitely be determined whether or not JOSEPH McCURRY prepared any of the above-listed signatures because of the limited amount of comparable known handwriting of McCURRY available.

There are listed below the names of the individuals whose names appeared on the petition but who signed their payroll marked with a witnessed "x":

James E. Moore	(Company B)
William Trumble	(Company B)
Henry Stoppel	(Company F)
J. Mahoney	(Company C)
William Etzler	(Company L)
Daniel Neelan	(Company H)
J. Adams	(Company H)
George W. Dewey	(Company H)
Thomas Lawhorn	(Company H)
Fredrick Deetline	(Company D)
William Hardden	(Company D)
James Hurd	(Company D)
James Seavers	(Company M)
Harrison Davis	(Company M)
George Weaver	(Company M)
William Rye	(Company M)
John Whisten	(Company M)

No known signatures could be located in the known specimens for comparison with the following signatures:

William Reese	(Company E)
William Channell	(Company H)
Edler Neis	(Company H)
Charles Fisher	(Company H)
M. J. Lacy	(Company H)
James Miles	(Company M)
Rollins Thorpe	(Company M)
William Williams	(Company M)

D-192503 DG
Page 4

Continued next page

There is insufficient comparable known handwriting
of any individual available in the known specimens to determine
whether or not any of these individuals wrote the petition
designated as Qc1.

The evidence submitted is being returned under
separate cover. No photographs have been made.

D-192503 DG
Page 5

BIBLIOGRAPHY, NOTES & INDEX

BIBLIOGRAPHY

Bradley, James H., "Journal of the Sioux Campaign of 1876." *Contributions to the Historical Society of Montana,* Vo. IV, 1896.

Brackett, Wm. S., "Custer's Last Battle." *Contributions to the Historical Society of Montana,* Vol. IV, 1903.

Carroll, John, ed., *The Benteen-Goldin Letters,* New York, 1974.

———.*Two Battles of the Little Big Horn,* New York, 1974.

du Bois, Charles G., *The Custer Mystery,* El Segundo, 1986.

Edgerly, W.S., "Narrative," *Research Review,* Little Big Horn Associates, Vol. III, Sept. 1986.

Frost, Lawrence A., *The Custer Album,* New York, 1954.

———.*Custer Legends,* Bowling Green OH, 1981.

Graham, W.A., *The Story of the Little Big Horn,* New York, 1926.

———.*The Custer Myth,* New York, 1953.

Horn, W. Donald, *Witnesses for the Defense,* Short Hills NJ, 1981.

Kuhlman, Charles, *Legend Into History,* Harrisburg, 1951.

Luce, Edward S., *Keogh, Comanche, and Custer,* St. Louis, 1939.

Miles, Nelson A., *Personal Recollections,* Chicago, 1896.

Stewart, Edgar I., *Custer's Luck,* Norman, 1955.

Vaughn, J.W. *Indian Fights,* Norman, 1966.

NOTES

PREFACE

[1] "The Custer Tragedy," by Fred Dustin, Ann Arbor, MI, 1939;"George Armstrong Custer," Dustin, Michigan History magazine, Vol. 30, No. 2, April-June, 1946. "Captain Benteen's Story of the Battle of the Little Big Horn June 25-26, 1876," by E.A. Brininstool, Hollywood CA, 1933; "Major Reno Vindicated," by Brininstool; From a Letter Written in 1925 by Col. W.A. Graham, U.S.A., with comments by E.A. Brininstool, Hollywood, 1935. "Glory-Hunter — A Life of General Custer," by Frederic F. Van de Water, Indianapolis and New York, 1934.

[2] "Personal Recollections," by General Nelson A. Miles, Chicago, 1896. These reminiscences of one of this country's most colorful army officers are a valuable contribution to the general history of the early frontier. It is written in a frank, modest style that will appeal to anyone interested in the subject.

INTRODUCTION

[1] General Kershaw's surrender at Sailor's Creek as quoted in a letter from J.T. Hill dated June 29, 1915. Custer Collection, Eastern Montana College, Billings, Montana. Sec. C A-19 C-1763
[2] Robert M. Utley and Wilcomb E. Washburn, *The American Heritage History of the Indian Wars* (New York, American Heritage Publishing Co., Inc., 1978), p. 301
[3] Colonel W.A. Graham, *The Custer Myth*, New York Bonanza Books, Copyright 1953, p. 180
[4] *Ibid.*, p. 180
[5] *Ibid.*, p. 181

SECTION I

[1] Lieutenant Edward S. Godfrey wrote in his journal, under the date, "Monday, July 24," nearly a month after the battle: "Col. Reno was placed in arrest by Genl. Gibbon." Again, on the following day we find the entry, "Col. Reno got a copy of the charges against himself. It all comes from Col. R. sending out some scouts as videttes Saturday eve, after we got into camp. I presume, however, that Col. Reno's manner, which is rather aggressive, has as much to do with the results, & he protested against the scouts being taken from the Regt."

It would seem from Godfrey's rather obscure reference to the incident that the source of Gibbon's action stemmed from an entirely unrelated event.

[2] The evidence was what appeared to the scouts to be a large herd of horses, which they correctly presumed to belong to the hostiles they were pursuing. [3] Not long after the battle it was determined that the Indians which had been seen near the divide, as well as those reported as "running like devils" by Gerard, belonged to a separate band of Cheyennes who never reached the big camp on the Little Big Horn. At the same time that Gerard saw the fleeing Indians Lieutenant De Rudio and others saw a cloud of dust in the valley over four miles distant. De Rudio later said that this dust cloud was then assumed to be caused by the main body of the hostiles as they made their escape. Actually it was caused by the Indians' pony herd. The Indians themselves said later that their first intimation that troops were nearby came only when Reno approached the southern end of the village. *The Custer Myth*, by Lt. Col. W.A. Graham, New York, 1953; p. 61, "Red Horse's Story;" p. 75, "Low Dog's Account;" p. 78, "Hump's story;" p. 79, "Iron Thunder's story."

[4] This, and all succeeding testimony, unless otherwise noted, is from, *The Official Record of a Court of Inquiry Convened at Chicago, Illinois, January 13, 1879, by the President of the United States, Upon the Request of Major Marcus A. Reno, 7th U.S. Cavalry, to Investigate His Conduct at the Battle of the Little Big Horn, June 25-26, 1876*, privately printed by Lt. Col. W.A. Graham, 1951. In this massive volume is found the most complete source of information on the Custer battle available. In the text of the Record the questioning and the testimony of the witnesses is presented in question and answer form. In order to add interest and emphasis, the author of this narrative has, in most cases, changed the form to that of ordinary conversation, at the same time presenting the testimony *verbatim*. Unless

otherwise stated, all such testimony as appears in this work is taken from the Official Record of the Inquiry.

[5] Official Report of Major Marcus A. Reno, July 5, 1876.

[6] *The Story of the Little Big Horn,* by Lt. Col. W.A. Graham, New York, 1926.

[7] One officer, obviously not briefed on Reno's "plan," did attempt to stop the retreating column. He was heard by Herendeen, though not identified in the scramble, to shout, "Company A men, halt! Let us fight them! For God's sake, don't run!" This officer was later identified as 2nd Lieutenant Charles Varnum of Company A. (*Ibid.,* p. 46 and *Custer in '76,* by Kenneth Hammer (Provo, 1976.) The statement was made within Reno's hearing, although Varnum was unaware of it. Reno replied, "I am in command here, Sir!"

[8] General Grant, though not a close personal friend of Custer, once wrote a letter of introduction for the young general: "This will introduce to your aquaintance Gen. Custer, who rendered such distinguished service as a cavalry officer during the war. There was no officer in that branch of service who had the confidence of Gen. Sheridan to a greater degree than Gen. Custer, and there is no officer in whose judgement I have greater faith than in Sheridan's. Please understand then that I mean by this to endorse Gen. Custer in a high degree."

General Sheridan, closer to Custer's rank and age, though his superior, entertained even keener appreciation for Custer's ability. After Grant and General Lee had agreed on the terms of surrender at Appamatox, Sheridan purchased the table on which the terms were written and presented it to Mrs. Custer with these words: "I respectfully present to you the small writing table on which the conditions for the surrender of the Confederate Army of Northern Virginia was written by Lt. Gen'l Grant & permit me to say, Madam, that there is scarcely an individual in our service who has contributed more to bring about this desirable result than your very gallant husband."

In 1869, at Fort Leavenworth, Sheridan paid this brief but revealing tribute to the 7th's youthful lieutenant-colonel: "Custer, you are the only man that never failed me." General A.B. Nettleson, who served as a colonel commanding the 2nd Ohio Cavalry Regiment of Custer's 3rd Cavalry Division, said: "Some of us were at first disposed to regard him [Custer] as an adventurer, a disposition which a sight of his peculiar dress and long locks tended to confirm. One engagement with the enemy under Custer's leadership dissipated all these impressions, and gave our new commander his proper place. Once under fire, we found that a master hand was at the helm, that beneath the golden curls and broadbrimmed hat was a cool brain and a level head.

"One thing that characterized Custer was this: having measured as accurately as possible the strength and morale of his enemy, and having made his own disposition of troops carefully and personally, he went into every fight with complete confidence in the ability of his division to do the work marked out for it. Custer's conduct in battle was characteristic. He never ordered his men to go where he would not lead, and he never led where he did not expect his men to follow ... He was a good disciplinarian, without being a martinet." (See also: *Witnesses for The Defense,* compiled by W. Donald Horn, Short Hill NJ. 1981).

[9] *The Custer Myth:* "General Godfrey's Narrative," footnote, page 142.

[10] *2Ibid.,* p. 335.

SECTION II

[1] The Benteen-Goldin Letters referred to in this section, were written by Benteen in retirement at his home in Atlanta, Ga., from 1891 until his death in 1896. These letters have been reproduced in full by John M. Carroll in his book, *The Benteen-Goldin Letters on Custer and His Last Battle,* New York, 1874. Hereinafter they will be referred to as B-G Letters. The reference for Note 1 is found on page 247.

[2] *Bugles, Banners and War Bonnets,* by Ernest L. Reedstrom, New York, 1977, p. 56.

[3] B-G Letters, p. 199.

[4] *Ibid.,* pp. 280-81.

[5] *Ibid.,* p. 199. It is of interest to note that despite the closeness between Benteen and his son, Major F.W. Benteen, the father never revealed the nature of his quarrel with Custer. In a letter to W.A. Falconer of Bismarck, North Dakota, dated May 23, 1930, Major Benteen wrote:

"You have asked me to tell you why he [Benteen] hated General Custer. I am sorry to say that I have not the remotest idea of the cause of this enmity between General Custer and my father. It was evidently a mutual dislike, and your guess is as good as mine as to what was the cause of the difference between them. It is very evident that whatever the cause originally was, neither ever forgave the other. Both of them may have been wrong, or both of them may have been right. Or one of them may have been right and the

other wrong, but in any event the difference between these two men seemed to be irreconcilable. As stated, I never knew the cause of the hatred. If I did know, I would not hesitate to tell you. I have no desire whatever to withhold the information, if I was in possession of it, but I simply do not know what the cause was."
It would seem that if any other cause existed, the younger Benteen would have know it.

[6] B-G Letters, p. 147.

[7] *Ibid.*, p. 154.

[8] Custer Myth, p. 227.

[9] B-G Letters, p. 207.

[10] *Custer Mystery*, by Charles G. du Bois, El Segundo, 1986, pp. 67-69.

[11] Hammer, p. 75.

[12] *Custer Myth*, p. 249.

[13] Hammer, p. 93, note 7.

[14] *Ibid.*, p. 93, note 11.

[15] *Custer Myth*, p. 291.

[16] *Ibid.*, p. 142.

[17] Dr. Charles Kuhlman, in his *Legend Into History*, (Harrisburg, 1951.) believed that Custer saw the troops on Weir Point and assuming them to be the reinforcements he had asked for, made a fatal deployment of his forces to accomodate Benteen's arrival. The theory can neither be proved or disproved. There is no doubt that Custer was alive at this time. Both Kate Bighead, a Cheyenne woman who watched the battle from a nearby ridge and reported on it with amazing accuracy, and Wooden Leg, a Cheyenne who participated in the battle, agree independently that the "long-distance firing" lasted about an hour and a half, and the subsequent battle on the battleridge lasted another forty minutes. (See *Wooden Leg*, p.230 and following). As Custer could not have reached the eastern extension of the battleridge (called "Calhoun hill") before 6:00 o'clock, the fighting on the western extension (called "Custer hill") would have ended about 7:00 p.m. The movement to Weir Point by Company D was completed by 5:00 o'clock, and the rest of the Reno-Benteen troops could not have joined them until about 6:30, before returning to Reno Hill from 7:00 to 7:30 p.m. Although Custer's movements may not have been visible to the troops on Weir Point,

Dr. Kuhlman's contention that Custer could see the troops outlined against the horizon is true beyond question, for the victorious Indians on Custer field saw them and rode after them, once they had finished with Custer.

[18] This imprecation was overheard by an officer who told it to General Nelson A. Miles. To protect the informant, Miles never revealed his identity. But if some doubt might exist that the words were actually spoken, there is supporting evidence to be found in one of Benteen's own admissions to Theodore Goldin. In a letter dated February 17, 1896, Benteen told of his visit to Custer's field on June 27, 1876. Returning from the scene he spoke to Lieutenant Edward Maguire of the Corps of Engineers and said, "By the Lord Harry, old man, 'twas a ghastly sight; but what a big winner the U.S. Govt. would have been *if only Custer and his gang could have been taken!*" (B-G Letters, p.271)

SECTION III

[1] A letter to Captain R.G. Carter, U.S. Army (Ret.) from General Edward S. Godfrey, dated April 14, 1925, had this to say: "There were several men of the 7th Cavalry at Soldiers Home and in Washington in 1921 & 22, who when asked if they had signed the petition denied ever having had such a thought, yet their signatures proved genuine. Not one would admit that he had signed, till shown his signature." (*The Custer Myth*, by Graham, p. 319). Colonel Graham, in commenting on this revealing statement, said, "General Godfrey is in error about these men at the Soldier's Home. They did not *deny* (italics by Graham) that they signed the Reno Petition. On the contrary, they said that did not *remember* it, and even after I showed them the signatures, which they said were their own, they did not recall it. Certainly there is the widest possible difference between *forgetting* an incident and *denying* that it ever occurred." (All Italics by Graham)
It was asking a great deal for men to testify to signing a document forty-nine years after the event. But if it can be said that their memories were faulty, so it can also be said that identifying an alleged "signature" as *theirs*, as opposed to their *name written by someone else*, is asking just as much of elderly men a half-century later.

[2] Col. W.A. Graham, in his book, *The Custer Myth*, pp. 283-84, lists all the names of the "signers" of the petition. Two of them were crossed out, leaving a total of 235 names. Graham had photostats of the signatures made in the 1920s and said the names were written in pencil and "are in many cases almost if not quite illegible." The names of 26 men not mentioned in the FBI report are misspelled. Nine of the 26 spelling errors are probably

indecipherable errors by Graham, such as "Labeldy" for "Lebeldy" and "Creswell" for "Criswell." That kind of error is understandable when we consider the condition of the pencilled document after so many years. However 17 of the names are so grossly misspelled that they are probably forgeries. Examples are "John Ryan" for "James Ryan," "Charles Zewengt" for "Charles Zervanst," and "Michael Crow" for "Michael Crowe."

SECTION IV

[1] As General Miles stated the case, "A general impression has gone abroad prejudicial to General Custer. He has been accused of disobeying orders, that he was too impatient, that 'he was rash', and various other charges have been. made, equally groundless and equally unjust, and all started and promoted by his enemies." (Miles, Gen. Nelson A., *Personal Recollections,* Chicago, 1896, p. 198).

[2] "It will be observed that General Custer was directed to move up the Rosebud in pursuit of the Indians. The next sentence, it will be noticed, leaves no question that it was expected that his command would come in contact with the Indians ... It is folly to suppose that either a small or large band of Indians would remain stationary, and allow one body of troops to come up on one side of it while another body came up on the other side and engaged it in battle." (Miles, *Personal Recollections,* p. 204).

[3] According to General Phil Sheridan, it was "... an almost totally unknown region, comprising an area of 90,000 square miles." (Brackett, William S., "Custer's Last Battle," reprinted in *Contributions to the Historical Society of Montana,* Vol. IV, 1903, p. 259.)

[4] Note the words, "sufficient reason." Shortly after the battle someone close to General Terry, probably a member of his staff, changed these words to read, *"absolute necessity, "* in an effort to strengthen the case against General Custer. Fortunately, and largely through the efforts of Col. W.A. Graham, the original copy written by General Terry was located in a warehouse at Fort Snelling, Minnesota, which proved that the phrase, "sufficient reason," was the correct version. (*Custer Myth* by Graham, pp. 155-56). It is not known which of Terry's officers were guilty of this forgery, but Col. Hughes, who had both motive (as Terry's brother-in-law) and opportunity (as aide de camp), ranks high on the list of suspects.

[5] Most white men of that day, and especially Army personnel, referred to the chief tributary of the Big Horn River (named for the Big Horn sheep) as the "Little Horn," rather than the more correct name, Little Big Horn.

[6] *Indian Fights,* by J.W. Vaughn, Norman OK, 1966.

[7] Here Godfrey interjected the words, "We never touched Tullock's Fork." (see Note 8, following).

[8] *The Two Battles of the Little Big Horn,* by John M. Carroll, Editor; New York, 1974. Appendix A, 142.

[9] Charlie (or Charley) Reynolds was one of the most prominent white scouts in the West during this period of our country's development. He had worked for General Custer on many previous occasions and was highly regarded by everyone who knew him. He was generally known by his nickname, "Lonesome Charlie."

[10] This stream is variously spelled "Tulloch" or "Tullock." To explain Herendeen's statement that "we were traveling in the direction of the head of the Tulloch," we must point out that the Rosebud, although flowing north, actually rises some distance west as well as south of its mouth on the Yellowstone. In following the stream Custer was marching south west, and the further he marched the closer he came to Tulloch's. (see map on page 00).

[11] Col. Graham said of him, "I never knew one more meticulously honest, or who had a higher regard for Duty, Honor and Country than did he." *Custer Myth,* p. 124.

[12] *Campaign Against the Sioux* by Col. Robert P. Hughes. This article, which first appeared in "The Journal of the Military Service Institution of the United States," Vol. 18, No. 74, January 1896, was reprinted as "Appendix I" in Col. Graham's *The Story of the Little Big Horn,* Harrisburg, 1926. Col Hughes served as Aide to General Terry during the Expedition of 1876. In addition he was the brother-in-law of Terry and was particularly dedicated to protecting Terry from criticism for Custer's defeat.

[13] Godfrey, Gen. E.S., "Custer's Last Battle," *Century Magazine,* Vol. 43, No. 3, January 1892.

[14] The various quotations from Col. Hughes are found in his article, "Campaign Against the Sioux," op. cit.

[15] *Two Battles,* Carroll, p. 145.

[16] Miles, Gen. N.A., *Personal Recollections,* pp. 205-06.

[17] All these quotes are from the Official Record of the Reno Court of Inquiry. op. cit.

[18] Godfrey, *Custer's Last Battle,* op. cit.

19 This was not the opinion of all of the officers with Gibbon and Terry. Lieutenant James Bradley, chief of scouts under Major Brisbin, and the leader of the advance party that discovered the bodies of Custer and his men, said in his diary, "Though it is General Terry's expectation that we will arrive in the neighborhood of the Sioux village about the same time and assist each other in the attack, *it is understood that if Custer arrives first he is at liberty to attack it at once, if he deems prudent.*" (italics mines, CdB). Bradley, "Journal of the Sioux Campaign of 1876 under the command of General John Gibbon," *Contributions to the Historical Society of Montana,* Vol. 2, 1896.

20 Hughes, *Campaign Against the Sioux,* op. cit.

21 Godfrey, *Custer's Last Battle.* op. cit.

22 Lieutenant Winfield Scott Edgerly, the first lieutenant of Co. D under Captain Weir, 7th Cavalry, made this statement in a newspaper article which appeared in the Leavenworth (Kansas) "Times," datelined Fort Yates, 18 Aug. 1881. The article is reprinted in full in Graham's, *The Custer Myth,* pp. 219-21.

23 This prescient officer was none other than the redoubtable Captain Benteen. When Custer told his officers that he doubted the scouts' statement that they had seen evidence of the hostiles' proximity, having observed nothing himself with the use of a binocular, Benteen later said, '. . . now strange perhaps to say, I did believe it: —— another 'Pre.' I knew it, because, why, I'd sooner trust the sharp eye of an Indian than to trust the pretty good binocular that I always carried; and I'd gotten that from experience. However, 'twasn't my 'chip in,' so I said nothing." (*Custer Myth,* p. 179). If this attitude of Benteen's seems strange, especially after Custer had solicited the advice of his junior officers, it must be remembered that Benteen was an extremely strange person. How else can we explain Benteen's reply at the Reno Court of Inquiry to a question regarding Custer's battle plans, "Not knowing where they [the Indians] were, I do not know whether there was any need of a battle plan." A strange admission, indeed, from a man who never lost an opportunity to criticize his dead commander.

24 Brigadier General George A. Forsyth, in his book, *The Story of the Soldier,* said, "In the opinion of the writer he [Custer] was within his orders, and fully justified from a military standpoint in doing so." (NY, 1900).

25 Although it is true that Custer was *not* discovered by the Indians from the village at this time, he was informed that such was the case.

²⁶ It is believed by some (this writer included) that a later division of the Custer battalion was made under the leadership of Captains George Yates and Myles Keogh, and that Custer, with his adjutant and non-commissioned staff, merely accompanied one of the two battalions. Of course there is no record of any such division today.

²⁷ Trumpeter John Martini, the only witness to Custer's words at this time, said that Custer shouted, "The Indians are asleep in their tepees!" As Martini spoke and understood very little English, it is most likely that he merely interpreted the more popular expression, "We've caught them napping" in this way.

²⁸ "Custer's order to Major Reno to move forward on the trail and attack the village, and that he would be supported by the other battalions, was a proper command, and did not imply that the supports would follow immediately in his footsteps. An attack by the battalion on his right or on his left or by both simultaneously, would be the most effective support he could have had." Miles, *Personal Recollections*, p. 207.

²⁹ The books cited as references in this work generally contain differing theories of the action on Custer field, Others include *Markers, Artifacts and Indian Testimony*, by Richard G. Hardorff, Short Hills NJ, 1985; *Custer's Luck*, by Edgar I. Stewart, Norman OK, 1955; *Legend Into History*, by Charles H. Kuhlman, Harrisburg, 1951, and *The Custer Mystery*, by Charles G. du Bois, El Segundo, 1986.

³⁰ Miles, *Personal Recollections*, p. 290.

³¹ Official Report of General Alfred E. Terry to General Sheridan, June 27, 1876.

³² Official Report of General of the Army William T. Sherman, 1876.

³³ "During the campaign every superior officer seems to have been haunted by the fear that the hostiles would run and get away from him if he did not divide his forces and surround them." Hyde, George E., *Red Cloud's Folks*, Norman OK. 1937.

³⁴ Brackett, *Custer's Last Battle*, op. cit., p. 262.

³⁵ "We could never understand why the soldiers left the timber for if they had stayed there the Indians could not have killed them." Grinnell, George B., *The Fighting Cheyennes*, NY, 1915, p. 337. In this same volume the author states, "For many years past the Northern Cheyennes whenever the Custer fight has been under discussion have expressed the opinion that if

Reno had remained in the timber the Indians could have done nothing with him." p. 344.

[36] "As he sent no despatch to Reno to change his movements, he evidently expected that officer to follow the trail and attack as he did in accordance with the then existing orders." Miles, *Personal Recollections*.

INDEX

Arickara scouts: 7, 16, 20

Battle of the Wilderness: 3
Bell, Capt. and Mrs. James: 24-25
Benteen, Capt. Frederick W.: 4-6, 9, 11, 19-
    21, 32, 41, 43-44, 47, 49-50, 54, 56-59, 61,
    74, 76-79, 81, 98-100, 103; assigned
    battalion, 32; at the morass, 35; description
    of him, 27; first meeting with Custer, 28-
    29; his Washita letter, 30-31; joins Reno
    on bluffs, 42; moves to Weir Point, 43;
    opinion of Reno's timber position, 9;
    receives message from Custer, 36-40; his
    reconnaissance to the left, 33-35; returns
    to Reno hill, 45-46
Benteen, Major F.W., Jr.: 98
"Big Bend" of the Rosebud: 64-65
Bighead, Kate: 99
Big Horn River: 55, 64, 101
Black Kettle, Cheyenne chief: 29
Bloody Knife, Arickara scout: 10
Bouyer, Michel "Mitch": 63, 68
Bradley, Lt. James: 103
Brininstool, E.A.: 95
Brisbin, Major James: 67-68, 72, 74, 76, 103

Calhoun Hill: 99
Camp Supply: 30
Camp, Walter: 39
Carter, Capt. R.G.: 100
Cedar Coulee: 79

Cheyenne Indians: 96, 104-105
Chicago (Ill.) *Times*: 27
Churchill, B.F.: 21
Civil War: 3, 18
Cooke, Lt. W.W.: 5-6, 36, 38-39, 78
Crook, Gen George: 65, 80
Crow Indians: 63
Crow's Nest: 4
Crow reservation: 63
Custer Battlefield: 43
Custer, Gen. G.A.: 6-7, 9, 16-19, 23-24, 28,
    33-34, 36-46, 49-50, 57, 61, 65, 70-76, 79,
    99-104; from Rosebud to Divide, 4; divides
    regiment, 5, 77; at the Washita, 29-30;
    confrontation with Benteen, 31-32; his
    orders reviewed, 62-64, 66-69; moves
    along bluffs, 78; causes of his defeat, 80-
    82; opinions of him, 97-98
Custer Hill: 44, 46, 99
Custer, Capt. Thomas W.: 79

Davern, Sgt. Edward: 5-6, 73
Davis Creek, MT: 65, 68, 75
De Gresse, W.J.: 30
De Rudio, Lt. Charles: 12-13, 44, 96
Dewey, Pvt. G.W.: 54
Dustin, Fred: 95

Edgerly, Lt. W.S.: 19, 38-39, 41, 44, 75, 103
Elliot, Maj. Joel: 29-31
Enlisted Men's Petition: 48-51, 55

Expedition of 1876: 3

Falconer, W.A.: 23, 98
Far West steamer: 61, 63
Federal Bureau of Investigation: 51-53, 55, 59, 85
Fisher, Pvt. Charles: 54-55
Fort Cobb, KS: 31
Fort Leavenworth: 97
Fort Meade, SD: 25
Fort Riley, KS: 28
Fort Snelling, MN: 101
Fort Yates, ND: 103
Frett, John: 21-22

Gerard, Fred: 5-6, 44, 73, 77, 96
Gibbon, Gen. John: 5, 9, 11, 46, 61, 64-65, 67, 70-72, 74, 96, 103
Gibson, Lt. Frank: 34-35
Gilbert, Lyman D.: 12-13, 22-23, 50
Godfrey, Lt. Edward: 9, 11, 19-20, 32, 43-46, 67-70, 72, 74, 96, 100, 102
Goldin, Pvt. Theodore: 28, 31, 35, 100
Goose Creek, WY: 65
Graham, Col. W.A.: 12, 23, 40, 95-97, 100-102
Grant, Pres. U.S.: 18, 50, 74, 97
Grey Horse Troop: 33

Haley, Timothy: 54
Hare, Lt. Luther: 8, 12, 14-15, 18, 44-45
Herendeen, George: 6-8, 11-12, 44, 67, 102
Heyn, 1st Sgt. William: 10
Hoover, J. Edgar: 52, 85
Houghtaling, Pvt. Charles H.: 55
Hughes, Col. Robert: 68. 71, 74-76, 101-102
Hunt, John: 54

"Indian Paradise": 64-65

Kanipe, Sgt. Daniel: 39, 41, 79
Kelly, James: 54
Keogh, Capt. Miles: 104
Klotzbucher, Pvt. Henry: 10-11
Kuhlman, Dr. Charles: 77, 99-100

Lawhorn, Thomas: 54
Leavenworth (KS) *Times*: 103

Lee, Lt. Jesse: 7-8, 11, 14-15, 17-19, 36-38, 40-41, 44-45
Le Forge, Thomas: 63
Little Big Horn Battle: 24, 48, 51, 58, 61, 80
Little Big Horn River: 4-6, 49, 61, 64, 68, 73-74, 82, 96, 101
Little Big Horn valley: 17, 32, 34, 74, 77
"Lone Tepee": 39, 77
Luce, Maj. E.S.: 42, 51-52

Maguire, Lt. Edward: 100
Marbrey, Lori: 56
Martini, Pvt. John: 36, 38-41, 78-79, 104
Mathey, Lt. Edward: 5, 23, 38, 40-41
McCurry, 1st Sgt. Joseph: 52-53, 57, 59
McDougall, Capt. Thomas: 5, 38-41, 77
Medicine Tail Coulee: 78-79
Miles, Gen. N.A.: 73, 79, 100-101
Mizpah Creek, MT: 3-4
Morass: 35-36
Moylan, Capt. Myles: 19, 21, 70

Nettleson, Gen. A.B.: 97
New York *Herald*: 34, 67
New York *Times*: 30

O'Hara, Sgt. Miles: 10
O'Ryan, William: 55

Porter, Dr. Henry: 5, 18, 73
Powder River Base: 55
Powder River, MT: 3-4
Pumpkin Creek, MT: 3-4

Reno Court of Inquiry: 7, 17, 20-21, 25, 27, 32, 35-36, 39-40, 42-45, 47-48, 50, 59, 96-97
Reno Creek, MT: 5, 32, 35, 65
Reno Hill: 12, 41-45, 78-79
Reno, Maj. M.A.: 6, 8, 10-12, 32, 35, 37, 42-45, 47-51, 56-59, 61, 74, 76-78, 81, 96-97, 104-105; his scout from Powder River, 3-4; assigned battalion, 5; ordered to charge Indians, 5-6; his description of charge, 7; moves to timber position, 9; retreats to bluffs, 10-11, 13-15; his opinion of Custer, 17-18; conduct on Reno Hill,

19-21; encounter with Frett, 21-23; his courts-
   martial, 24-25
Reno, Official Report: 21, 45
Reynolds, Charlie: 8, 68, 102
Rosebud River, MT: 4, 61-66, 68-70, 73, 75,
   101

St. Louis (MO) *Democrat*: 30
St. Paul, MN: 24
Seventh Cavalry: 3-4, 49, 62
Sheridan, Lt. Gen. Philip: 18, 66, 70, 74, 80,
   97, 101
Sheridan, WY: 65
Sherman, General W.T.: 50, 57, 74, 80-81
Shields, Pvt. William: 56
Smith, Capt. E.W.: 61
Smith, Pvt. George: 10
Sterland, Walter: 55
Sturgis, Gen. S.D.: 25

Terry, Gen. A.H.: 46, 61-67, 69-75, 80,
   101-103
Terry, Official Report: 66
Tongue, River, MT: 3-5, 72

Townsend, E.D.: 47-48, 52, 85
Tolson, Hillory A.: 85
Tulloch's Creek, MT: 66-69, 102

Van De Water, Frederic: 95
Varnum, Lt. Charles: 18, 97

Wallace, Lt. George: 5-6, 12, 75
Walter, Aloyes L.: 54-55
War Department: 58
Washita Battle: 17, 29-31
Washita Letter: 30-32
Washita River, KS: 29
Weir Point: 42-43, 45-46, 99
Weir, Capt. Thomas: 32, 35, 38-41, 43-44,
   103
White, Sgt. Charles: 10
Windolph, Sgt. Charles: 54-55
Wolf Mountains, MT: 4, 32, 64, 76, 80
Wooden Leg, Cheyenne warrior: 99

Yates, Capt. George: 34, 104
Yellowstone River, MT: 4, 62, 64, 102

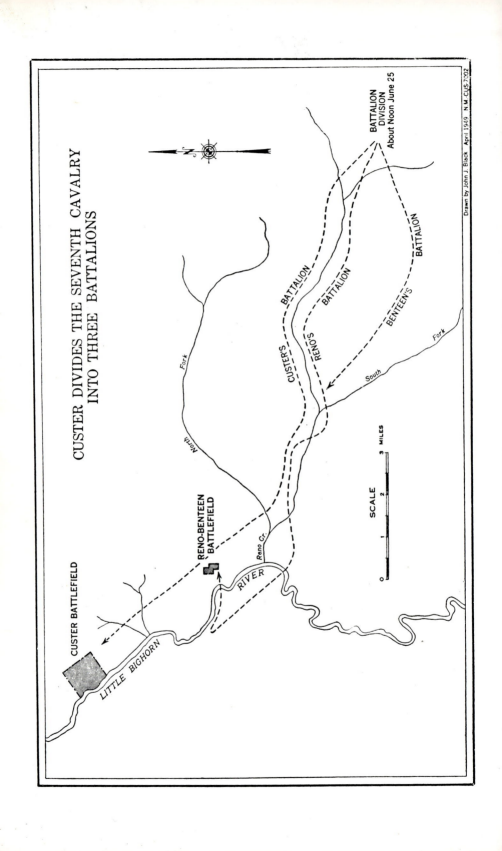

CUSTER DIVIDES THE SEVENTH CAVALRY
INTO THREE BATTALIONS

CUSTER BATTLEFIELD

RENO-BENTEEN
BATTLEFIELD

LITTLE BIGHORN

RIVER

Reno Cr.

North Fork

Fork

CUSTER'S BATTALION

RENO'S BATTALION

BENTEEN'S BATTALION

South Fork

BATTALION DIVISION
About Noon June 25

SCALE

0   1   2   3 MILES

Drawn by John J. Black April 1949 N.M. CUS.7002